SEASONS OF A SPIRITUAL LIFE

SEASONS OF A SPIRITUAL LIFE

A. LYNN SCORESBY

Bookcraft
Salt Lake City, Utah

Library of Congress Catalog Card Number: 86-70804
ISBN 0-88494-594-4

First Printing, 1986

Printed in the United States of America

To everything there is a season, and a time
to every purpose under the heaven.
—Ecclesiastes 3:1

CONTENTS

Chapter 1

THERE IS A
SEASON

I once went on a guided tour of the Louvre, the famous art museum in Paris. I walked through long halls viewing historic sculptures and other acclaimed works of art. I entered a large room where, to my right, the way had been secured by two rows of crimson velvet rope held by brass clasps attached to several pillars which stood a few feet apart. The tour guide explained that the room contained the da Vinci collection. There, among several paintings, was the *Mona Lisa*, perhaps Leonardo da Vinci's most famous painting. I was delighted at my fortune to have such a good view of the work. I was a small-town boy and not well educated or sophisticated in the world of art.

I began to listen attentively as the guide explained that da Vinci painted in a style which incorporated an isosceles triangle. As the guide explained the style in detail, using the *Mona Lisa* and another painting, *The Last Supper*, I could not take my eyes from the paintings. I could still see each painting as a scene familiar to me, but I now also viewed it in a new and different way.

I became so engrossed in what the paintings looked like and how the artist had organized them that I

1

failed at that time to consider something vital. A picture is a picture because it is enclosed and separated from other images. It is portrayed within a border or frame which suggests to those viewing it that the inside is a presentation of a concept representing a person, an event, or a landscape. Looking at the picture, one is first caught up in a general impression without recognizing that it is the frame that directs his eyes where to look and appreciate.

I have often reflected upon the lessons learned from this experience. It seems to me that they have an important application for those who are interested in understanding spiritual things.

It is not always easy to determine what is most important for us to learn from what happens to us in this life; it is not always easy to see our experiences in ways that will help us grow. Sometimes we need a guide to direct where to look and appreciate, much as a frame directs attention to a picture. Sometimes we need to recognize that what is obvious to us may not be as important as an underlying meaning.

The gospel of Jesus Christ gives us a framework for discovering the spiritual significance of the events of our lives. And it suggests to us that divine instruction is ongoing between God and humankind. When we learn to listen to and benefit from this instruction, we can learn what is most important for our spiritual growth and we can be more adequately prepared for a future existence.

Our Father, who has dominion over all things, instructs us in several ways. If we listen for and heed the whisperings of the ''still, small voice'' within us, we can learn to recognize his direction. Our Father further instructs us through a form of communication referred to as prayer. Instruction has also been sent to us in revelations and visions to persons called to represent the Father. His most important representative was his own Son, who lived among us and revealed to us the personality of our Eternal Father.

The life of Jesus Christ, the Son of God, gave us the example, the standard by which we can judge life's experiences. The gospel he taught gave us the framework for perceiving the connections between this life and the life where God dwells. Further, because in the learning process of mortality we damage our souls and those of others, this Son was to purchase with his life a way to repair that damage. Because of his important role, we are counted righteous when we show faith in him and do all important things in his name.

It is given to us all to have certain times in our lives that stand out from our ordinary existence, certain times when we are tried or challenged or caused to reflect. We may regard such times as mere coincidences of mortal life, but if we do we will miss important spiritual lessons that these times present to us. At such times spiritual things can be brought into sharper focus, illuminating our understanding of the eternal.

If we appreciate that some life experiences are given in order that we can be partakers of heavenly things, and if we seek for the spiritual meaning in these experiences, we grow in our knowledge about God and the place we will someday live. More important, knowing our Father has sent messages and feeling their validity will change us; we will be able to live as he lives.

We know that such experiences are not constant. When they have passed, we reengage this world, and that which was spiritual can only be treasured in our memories to be privately pondered and rehearsed for solace and growth. What do we lose if we are looking elsewhere when these times come, if we see only what appears on the surface of our experience? Like the unprepared viewer of the work of art, we will be unable to understand the message of the Creator. We will be like those of whom it was said that "seeing they might not see, and hearing they might not understand" (Luke 8:10). We can conclude that it is best to be ever watchful, so we may recognize the spiritual seasons of our lives that will teach us of our Father and his life.

Recognizing Spiritual Seasons

Spiritual seasons can come quietly, or they can come dramatically. Most are brief. Every person has them, and though the nature of the experiences may vary widely, the spiritual meanings are surprisingly similar for everyone. The seasons described in this book are experienced by nearly everyone throughout life.

My mission president stressed that an effective teacher was one who was able to use the investigator's personal experiences to illustrate gospel principles. In this way, a true principle could be received by each person according to his own understanding. We see this same idea in the teaching of the Savior, and especially in the variety of methods he used in miraculous healings. For some, healing seemed to be purely a divine gift. For others, healing was accompanied by forgiveness of sins. Still others were told that their healing was the result of their own faith in the power of the Lord. In each case, his discerning spirit enabled Jesus to understand the precise way to use a person's background to teach and bless him.

As a teacher of a Gospel Doctrine Sunday School class, I invented an exercise to teach about the Savior's mission. Without telling the class my objective, I divided them into two groups and gave the following written instructions to each group: "You are to create a plan to help you know whether or not you can completely trust the rest of those in the class. Then select one of your group to present this plan, and persuade the others to accept it."

The groups discussed and formulated their plan in a few minutes. The representative of the first group arose and gave a "hard-sell" presentation. Members of the class raised a polite question or two and then nothing more was said. Then the person selected from the second group stood and simply said, "I have a plan that will allow all to be trusted if you will follow after me." The effect of this statement was electric. Some wanted to know why we should follow him. One person said that the first plan had more advantages. At first, I thought everyone saw through this little exercise and was pretending just to go along. Some, however, became genuinely exercised and had to be quieted, so I knew they had not discovered the unseen purpose. As I watched, I soon had a hard time swallowing, and my eyes filled with tears. I realized I had inadvertently exposed some of the human frailties that led to the Savior's rejection by his friends. After talking it over, the class left quite subdued and thoughtful.

I have frequently thought since then about how easy it can be to miss the spiritual significance of "ordinary" experiences. God does indeed send messages that only his faithful can receive. If we react to our experiences only in terms of their worldly facades, we may miss the messages meant for us. We must go beyond the facade and meditate, pray, and listen to our discerning spirit. In this way, we find the truth.

Benefitting from the Spiritual Seasons

If we recognize them, spiritual seasons can benefit us in many ways. We receive inspiration and comfort from them. Through them, we may learn information that guides us in our decisions, and through them we can also feel the careful sensitivity of heavenly parents, shown in the precision of spiritual messages designed especially for us. Through them, we know we are loved.

I believe there is still another purpose for these experiences. Spiritual seasons aid in the development we must experience as a part of mortal life. Development is the physical, mental, social, and spiritual progress we make as we grow. It is so natural that we usually take it for granted except when it is prevented by disability or abruptly ended in "untimely" death. Yet, if we stop and notice, we will realize that attention to growth fills our lives in numerous ways. We might hear or say "I can't believe time passes so fast." "The children are growing up too quickly." "When do you plan to retire?" "The older I get the slower I go." "Wouldn't it be great to be young again?" We need only recall any recent conversation to see how often we discuss the changes that take place as time passes.

Development is so intimately woven into the fabric of our thought and language that we sometimes forget to consider to what end we are developing. Latter-day Saints believe we are on earth to gradually become more like our eternal parents. Our development toward this end is more rapid if we avoid pitfalls and distractions that tempt us away from our path. Left alone and separated from the sustenance found in the premortal life, we might wander or weaken. Spiritual seasons are generated to nurture our spirit, to enable us occasionally to partake of a heavenly gift that creates a new spark of spiritual light to send us forward again.

The early years of life are the time when we struggle to learn how to live in a physical world. Ironically, we find our senses can be relied upon because they are wonderfully adapted to this place. In the process of learning how to use them, we often come to believe that knowledge about the world and our success in it depends on what we can see, hear, taste, touch, and smell. Yet, we are told that all that can be known through our physical senses is temporary, that to progress we must develop a spiritual or soul voice that we rely on more than our physical senses. As we develop this capacity we are in a better position to benefit from the spiritual experiences given us by God.

Spiritual seasons stimulate the growth of our inner sense. They quicken and refine our appreciation for truth. We are then drawn to truth and can, if we choose, come to love it.

In spiritual seasons we can learn of God and draw ourselves close to him. There is a season for everything, and some seasons are not easy to endure. If we have the world set in our hearts, they shake us. Without them we could not find "the work that God maketh from the beginning to the end" (Ecclesiastes 3:11). Other seasons will be less burdensome to us, but they will obligate us more because of what we have learned in these seasons of growth. But in all seasons those who have ears to hear or eyes to see will know what is taught and will grow.

Chapter 2

THE
PROVING

I did not hurry, because the sounds had not the sharp edge that pain gives to a child's cry. When I turned the corner from the hallway into the family room, I stopped before Jeremy saw me, and watched to learn the reasons for his small distress. I found him crawling toward a couch. He pulled himself into a standing position and then let go of the couch, trying to walk. At this point, he fell quite solidly to the floor and cried out. Thinking that the minor pain from the fall would end his attempts, I was surprised when he crawled over and tried again—with the same result. He repeated this sequence several times. His legs simply were not ready, even if his mind thought they should be.

From infancy on, all humans show an inherited motivation to become more competent. As we physically mature, there is noticeable effort on our part to do much more than lie around and sleep. Rolling over, sitting up, crawling, standing, and walking begin a sequence of growth that continues throughout life. Human infants also exhibit a great curiosity about what they see, hear, taste, smell, and touch. It is as if everything must be known for what it is or what it can do. Young children begin life by proving this world and the people in it. They seem to be deciding whether mortality is a good place to be. And, if it is a good place, then they want to know how to survive in it.

Recent advances in child psychology are producing support for the concept of eternal personalities. For many years, behavioral scientists believed that memory and intelligence were the result of repeated encounters with a stimulus. The brain, like a camera, was thought to take sensory pictures that remained in previously unfilled brain cells. Now, however, there is mounting evidence that an infant's mind is not a total blank ready to begin learning. It is, instead, organized and intelligent from birth, and it begins immediately to organize and interpret what it perceives. When given exactly the same new sounds or sights, children will interpret them in individual ways, based on their own style of thought or what they have obviously known previously. This means that the human mind is learning only what it does not already know. It also interprets and applies what is already known. This is the difference between discovering and recognizing. We know now that children recognize as well as discover.

The urge to comprehend and interpret, to prove the world, seems to characterize us throughout life. This urge drives us in our careers, in our relationships with others, in our evaluation of ourselves. The urge to prove the world is perhaps most apparent in the quests for knowledge of the explorer, the scientist, and the scholar. But to some degree, all of us are proven in roles such as parent, friend, church worker, neighbor, and family member.

Years after that earlier experience with Jeremy, I sat by his side helping him with his school work. He was in the fourth grade. He was a big boy, larger than most of his friends. But his size was no advantage when it came to long division. As I watched him do his homework, I noticed he had difficulty with basic multiplication. I thought this was the reason for his problems with division. While I was thinking about ways to help him, he turned to me and said, "Dad, I am the dumbest kid in class." "Why do you think that?" I asked. "Because I don't get my work done in school like the rest of the kids do," he replied. His sad expression affected me, and I knew he felt what he said. I told him that part of his situation was my fault because I had not realized that he needed some extra help. "No," he said, "I'm just dumb." "You are not dumb!" I protested. Attempting to dissuade him, I raised my tone of voice and emphatically said, "You are one of my smartest boys." I could tell he was not convinced.

While trying to think of something more persuasive, I suddenly remembered my experience watching him try to walk. I told him about it. "Everybody faces challenges," I said. "You had to prove you could walk, and you were not satisfied when you couldn't. Now you are facing another challenge. Prove to yourself you can do it. It might take some hard work, but you and I can do it." I watched the expression of hurt and anger soften, and realized my statement had had some effect, at least for a while. I knew, however, that more than words were necessary. He would have to work hard enough to actually succeed. There was no substitute.

I reflected upon this experience and thought about the great influence life's challenges have on all of us. If we meet them well, we prove to ourselves that we are able. If we fail to meet what is thrust upon us or what we find in life's path, we shall prove ourselves inadequate. Jeremy had proven to himself that he was dumb because he had convinced himself he could not do long division. I was confident, however, that he could succeed in doing his math and prove himself able if he would expend the necessary amount of effort. The choice was completely his. He was in a season of proving.

It took both of us several nights of persistent work, but because of that work Jeremy now believes he can do whatever his teacher assigns. Like all of us, he will find that life provides many seasons of proving. Some we plan for; others come as surprises. The proving of ourselves, either as capable or inadequate, is an unavoidable part of life. We will interpret virtually everything we do to reflect something about ourselves. It seems so much a part of everyone's existence that it must be a condition inherent in mortality.

Standards

Seasons of proving can take place at any time, and most of us have more than one. A first important season of proving comes to us during early childhood. We prove ourselves to parents or others who take care of us. Our feelings about our success in this season influence us greatly throughout our lives. Witness these words of Paul Newman: "I think my father thought I was a lightweight. I am sorry he died before I could prove to him otherwise."

We descend from ancestors who made decisions that affect us, and we come before descendants who will be influenced by us. Each generation transmits to the next its traditions, its values, its personal memories, and its knowledge of life. I follow parents who knew of hard work, who wanted more education, and who were committed to their religion. These three elements were woven into the fabric of our family life. Along with love and respect, they were what I thought life was all about. Because my parents valued these things, they became the proving arena for me. There is nothing in particular that makes these values better than some others. But because my parents held to them, I was to be proven by them.

When I was about ten years old, I began to beg my father to let me drive the tractors, as my older brothers did. For a year I begged, and then finally, out of necessity, my father told me one day to drive the "M" to the "sixteen acres." The "M" was an International or Farmall tractor, and it was the favorite of my brothers. I drove the tractor slowly and carefully down the gravel road to the field where my father waited. When I stopped, he climbed on and began to drive. "I'll show you how," he said. For a few rounds (up and down the field) he drove and explained to me what he was doing. Then he changed places with me as I drove the tractor. I soon learned how to cultivate potatoes.

Designed to eliminate the newly growing weeds, the cultivator hung onto the sides of the tractor and was fixed with tools that dug close to the small plants. Because the "diggers" threw dirt and might cover the plants, the driver of the tractor had to go very slowly. To ensure that I would go the correct speed, my father showed me the proper gear and location of the throttle, telling me to leave them in place. As a further precaution against being covered, the plants passed through "shields" or tin plates, six inches apart and about two feet long on each side of the tractor. This passage was so narrow that the driver had to look steadily at the shields in order to keep from digging up the plants.

As we practiced, my father adjusted all the parts of the cultivator until the result satisfied him. After riding with me several rounds, he climbed off the tractor and watched me while I proudly, and I thought deftly, moved up and down the rows. After seeing that I could "handle" it, he stopped me. He told me to keep going, and that he would return at lunch time.

In my memory's eye, I can still see him driving away. I felt grown up and important. I started the tractor and began. I noticed that people seemed to be looking at me, and as each car drove by I felt sure that our neighbors were wondering how so young a person could be doing such significant work and were marveling at the fine job I was doing all by myself.

Soon, however, this feeling was less significant to me than my awareness of how awfully slow I had to travel. So slowly was I going that I sometimes tired of watching the potatoes go between the shields, and my mind wandered. It was then I learned that if the driver digs up the potatoes on the right side of the tractor, the plants on the left side are also ruined.

I tried to think of things to keep from being bored, so that I could keep my eyes on the task. I sang songs; I thought of stories; I talked to imaginary people. After doing all these things, I found myself still in the field, cultivating potatoes, going slowly up and slowly down. I looked at what had been done and saw that it was very little compared to what was still to be done. I remember the feelings of frustration rising within me as I realized the hours that this work was going to take. I was so angry that I threw a small tantrum and stamped hard on the tractor to vent my feelings.

I am not sure how long it took me to think of it, but I eventually decided that the cultivator needed adjustment. I stopped the tractor and, with wrenches in hand, climbed off. I raised some implements and lowered others. As I started off again, I could see that what was being done was not quite right, so I stopped to adjust things again. This process of adjusting and readjusting the cultivator occupied me for quite some time. As the feeling in my stomach signaled that noon approached, I began to watch for my father's arrival. I had done very little actual cultivating, which was all right, of course, because I had had to adjust the cultivator.

When Dad returned to take me home, he noticed that I had not done much. He mentioned just that and nothing else. I was relieved that he hadn't scolded me, and I turned my thoughts to the meal I knew awaited me at home; I remember that it tasted very good. After eating, I was playing with my friends when I heard my Dad say, "Well, I guess we had better go." My heart, stomach, and all other vitals sank as one within me. I tested Dad a little to see if he was truly committed, discovered he was, and soon found myself once again going slowly, ever so slowly, up and down the rows with the potatoes moving through the shields one by one.

I soon decided once again to stop and adjust the cultivator, and for a while this strategy relieved my boredom as well as it had in the morning. But eventually I found that guilt reduced the value of this distraction. I could see then that I was left to one course of action, and in my decision to follow it, I learned something of great benefit to me: The only way to cultivate potatoes is to go up two rows, go down two rows, go up two rows more, down two more, and so on until all the rows are finished.

Dad had more than one field, and I learned that summer to go from one to another, all summer long, until the potato vines grew too large to permit the tractor to pass through without damaging them. When that day came, it was better than Christmas, but I did not overly expose my joy to others.

The next summer, I was again faced with the same task. To relieve my boredom, I caught on to an interesting idea. If I saw the task as drudgery, it was boring and difficult. But if I looked on it as a challenge, I found ways to enjoy it. I was motivated to think about becoming as good as I could become. I tried to keep my rows straight and hit all the weeds, and I developed a system of turning that reduced the amount of shoveling at irrigation time. Soon I gained a modest reputation as a "good" cultivator and even won a grudging compliment from a usually undemonstrative uncle. As I grew older, I even began to look forward to those times alone when I could think and be at peace with myself. Today such time is a luxury I seldom have.

As I grew, my work improved. I received more attention and compliments from my father. "You're doing a man's work," he would say, rubbing his hand through my hair. For a twelve-year-old boy, that was high praise. It was in this and other ways that I was proven by my parents' expectations. They and I both knew that I could work like they worked. And it was the same with their religion, their emphasis on education and learning, and their love and respect. They created the tasks for me that enabled me to find success, though these tasks also risked failure. I came to be proven by a mission, by the challenges of a temple marriage, by a college education, by development of talents, and by service to others. As my parents' child, I tried to master what they set before me while they loved and taught me along the way. I knew of no alternative. This was life.

My early proving experiences marked my life, and I have benefitted from them continually. As a missionary, I was surprised to learn that some companions could not or would not get up at six o'clock, learn their discussions, or do contacting work. I was thankful then for the "M" and for the cultivator. I knew how to work, and although I may not have been the smartest Elder, I could get things done. Nothing I ever encountered on my mission was worse than cultivating or hauling hay.

Much later in my life, after I had finished my graduate studies, I was contacted by a woman who asked me to help her husband. He was not able to finish his graduate degree even though he had been a brilliant student. He told me that he had completed his course work and had been working on his dissertation for several years without completing it. Each time he began to write it, he was distracted by something. A dissertation, I knew, was not easy to write. Depending on the field of study, it might be as long and detailed as a textbook.

To compound his problems, this man had collected a large amount of information that had to be organized. Each time he began to write, he would find something unorganized, stop writing to attend to that, and never get back to the writing. He did not get the type of job he wanted because he had not obtained his doctor's degree; his family was in a difficult financial condition, his wife was unhappy, and he was depressed.

During the course of our association, I had asked him to tell me exactly what happened as he began to write. "I go into my office," he said, "and get my papers, notecards, and everything organized." "Then what?" "Well, I might start writing and need some notecard to quote from. In the search for it, I'll find something else, and before long I have forgotten about writing." "If you recognize this, why don't you do something about it?" I asked. "I guess because I get so discouraged about not having written anything, I don't feel like going on," he answered.

I knew how he felt. I had become so discouraged while writing my dissertation that often I did not care if I ever saw it again. But once you start a project like this, you cannot let go of it. If you do, it will make a failure of you. As long as you are at least trying to write it, the ugly spectre of inadequacy has not quite yet materialized. But the longer you go without doing it, the more afraid you become that you cannot. This fear can cripple the motivation to write.

He and I talked together, and I made a few preliminary suggestions, which did not help. Then one day as he was telling me of one of his attempts to write, I recognized his problem. I looked steadily at him and said, "You are fixing your cultivator." His expression showed that my statement was as strange to him as if I had said it in a foreign tongue. I had meant for it to get his attention, but it had so puzzled him that he thought I had lost contact with reality. I told him of my youthful experience, and when he understood, he nodded his agreement. "My father was quite old when I was born," he began. "When I was a boy, he did not want to do active things. When I would run or something, he would say, 'Come and sit by me, now; we don't want to get too tired.' I would guess," my friend said, "I have never had to work much to succeed."

He had proven himself according to what his father expected of him, just as I had been proven according to what my father expected of me. His proving qualified him in many areas, but did not help him perform well enough to resolve depression and fear.

I asked him if he could tell me some of the things he had always wanted to do but had never done. Without a moment's hesitation, he said, "Climb Timpanogos." "What else?" I asked. He named two or three other challenges. We made plans, and he promised to do each one.

An outsider would not have seen any relationship between writing a dissertation and climbing a mountain. Truthfully, I am not sure I did either, but I had a hunch. My friend did all he promised, and the success of it was written all over his face. Something changed within him. I thought I knew what it was. Coincident to this time, he received word that his graduate committee was again prepared to supervise his work. One day while puttering in his office, he began to write. As I recall, he finished writing his dissertation and satisfactorily completed his examination all within six or seven weeks.

When we know we have achieved and proven ourselves by the accomplishment, we more confidently face challenges in the future. Children whose parents expect little or who expect unreasonable and unrealistic performance are unfortunate. Children who have conflict with parents and rebel against them are often rejecting what their parents hope for them. There is very little that children can do to prove themselves without the involvement of their parents or other adults. Finding no real way to measure their existence, they usually experiment. Some try different religions. Others try out alternative life-styles. Most acquire a detached view of themselves and of other people. They make few commitments except to cynicism. Children of these parents can remain unproven all of their lives—not because of their inability, but because there was nothing to meet, nothing to beat, nothing to endure, and nothing to sacrifice for. There was nothing. And they make themselves into very little. Some, however, go on away from parents and struggle to prove themselves elsewhere—to a husband, a business partner, a friend. Seasons of proving continue until each of us has faced challenges and opportunities and feel proven by them.

Overcoming a Habit

"It tastes good, it looks good, and I want to eat it." These were the thoughts of a pretty and petite twenty-year-old girl who was about to eat a piece of apple strudel. The thoughts seem commonplace; they were not commonplace to her. They represented one side of a most intense struggle. For several years, this girl's mother had closely supervised her eating habits, frequently criticizing her if she ate too much. She became fearful of the guilt criticism brought, and she began to sneak away and eat by herself. Weight gain was to be avoided at any cost, so she often starved herself for long periods. These periods were followed by an eating binge that equalized things somewhat.

One day she learned from a friend at school that vomiting after each meal was a good way to stay slender. The added advantage of vomiting was that she could eat as much as she wanted. She began a process of starving, binge eating, and vomiting. This, of course, produced more guilt and secretive behavior. She began to steal food from her parents' refrigerator, and she learned to lie to hide her habits. Once begun, her activities continued and increased until she was purging her food an average of eight times a day, or once every two hours. She would panic whenever she felt too full, but she refused to talk to anyone about her problem. She was clearly risking her health; she had acquired an eating disorder called bulimia.

At the time of her encounter with the apple strudel, she was participating in a program designed to change what she was doing. To establish some confidence, she had been asked to set small goals each day to see if she could keep them. On this particular morning she wrote the goal that she would not eat any desserts that day. She had caught herself when she was cutting a piece of apple strudel. She told the following story: "I stopped for a second and asked myself if I would rather have peace of mind knowing that I had done what I had said I would do. I put the dessert down and left. It was a while before I realized that I had chosen a good feeling over something I had wanted to eat. I am not sure why it was right to do that, but I know it was."

She made her choice between something physically satisfying and an intangible feeling. She had chosen to strengthen her character by producing the sensation of self-control. She was faced with a dilemma that would prove her limits, her strengths, and her moral courage. Her struggle had just begun, but she was demonstrating to herself that she could establish self-control in order to have self-respect rather than give in to the urge to eat excessively. Her objective was simply to feel better about herself, and to do that she would have to eliminate the binge eating and vomiting.

As I listened to her story, I thought to myself that she was at least fortunate enough to be able to identify what her choices were. Others I knew did not see as clearly. I thought of men and women who had confused happiness with wealth and prestige. I knew students who had been confused about grades and had cheated on tests, robbing themselves of something else. I believe that every person will be confronted with choices—understood or not—between something physical, something external and concrete in nature, and something unseen but felt within. It is the proving of a character, a soul, and an eternal destiny.

The Parents' Test

I had often heard a friend of mine speak of the difficulty and hurt brought about by premarital pregnancies. Among his comments during public speeches, he sprinkled references to the embarrassment and sadness such events brought to the parents of those involved. He and his wife have lived exemplary lives themselves and are, in my opinion, among the kindest and most generous people I know. For many years they have held church and civic positions, and they are well known and well liked. He is very successful in his business and is embarrassed about it as shown by his attempts to minimize his success. His sense of pride was built on the quiet confidence of his successful life, and he commands the respect of his acquaintances.

It was in this setting of social prominence and strong religious conviction that a season of proving came for this man and his wife. I learned about it in a conversation following an early morning game of golf. He was more quiet than usual as we played, but I did not suspect anything until he started to talk. I could tell that it was not easy for him, but I saw that he had selected me to hear his voice tell the story. The story itself was quite brief, but it contained years and years of feeling. It was about his son who had, a day or so before, told his father about his girlfriend's pregnancy.

As I listened to my friend and felt his sadness, I noticed that my attention changed from hearing the story to observing how this good person was facing the situation. To my surprise, he was closely watching me as he told his story. I suppose I was a trial run for him, and he was testing the experience. As I watched I could see the emotions displayed on his face flow with the reluctance of a private person who is exposed without wanting to be. He searched for a clear reaction from me, and I felt an increasing need to find the right words to say.

He told me of their great hurt as he and his wife discussed their son; he described the first rush of anger at the boy and the irrational desire to blame the girl. He told of his wife's tears and sleepless nights, and his own preoccupation with the situation. As his voice grew tired, I thought I saw resignation and despair. I blurted out, "When are you taking them to dinner?" He looked at me for a long moment. At first I thought my impulsiveness had overstepped his confidence in me. He then looked down at the ground, and back to me before saying, "How did you know we were doing that?" After another silent moment, I said, "Because you are the kind of person who will love your son and be more concerned about him than you will worry about yourself." They had planned to take the two young people out to dinner and discuss ways to provide support for them as they started their marriage plans. In a short while, parents and children would, as a family, face the public nature of their circumstance.

He relaxed as he found that his decision in a strange and difficult situation was understood by someone else. He probably has forgotten this incident. I have not. I was an observer of a time in someone's life when personal sadness and the threat of public embarrassment were made secondary to a parent's desire to support his child. He and his wife have done well in one of their seasons of proving.

Whether in sustained and quiet reinforcements of right choices, or in dramatic confirmation of successfully met major challenges, we see constant evidence that we are being proven here, for reasons we may not fully understand. We can know in our private thoughts that our experiences have a meaning beyond the events themselves. In our seasons of proving we can recognize the very challenges and temptations required to strengthen us in some particular way. Could it be that some prearranged plan is at work? Do our very weaknesses lead us to dilemmas that give us a chance to grow? I have seen so much human trouble that I think this might be the case. What we haven't mastered at the time of birth will be challenged during mortality so that we can continue to progress. God's works are made manifest to us in the conditions we face here.

We may not always appreciate the tasks given us to prove ourselves until they have passed. But we must remember that ultimately it is against God's standards, not man's, that we must be proven, and God's ways are not always immediately understood by mortals. If we listen to the inner voice, however, and learn to follow divine instruction, we can find God's way, step by step, and increase in faith each time we struggle and conquer in a season of proving.

Chapter 3

PURPOSES
AND
PREPARATION

I watched my eleven-year-old son participate in his first Little League basketball game. I was probably more excited than he was, but I was able to avoid showing it. As I watched, I noticed that he was not able to dribble with his left hand very well and, as a result, missed several opportunities during the game. To help, I played with him two or three evenings during the next few weeks and, without telling him, played so that he had to dribble with his left hand. Finally, the game came when he stood holding the ball, the defender on his right side, and he dropped the ball to the floor with his left hand and dribbled quickly to the basket, completing an exciting play. (At least it excited him and his dad.)

As I left the game thinking smilingly about this small event, I felt a thrill of insight. My son had been prepared without knowledge of the purpose, but he had recognized the right time and simply acted as he had practiced. I knew the purpose for his preparation but he did not. We were both excited about his having made the basket, but I was also happy that his preparations achieved the purpose. I wondered if an Eternal Father was preparing sons and daughters who didn't know his purposes.

To act according to a purpose means to act intentionally in harmony with the future. What we do is not *caused* by our purposes, though it may *serve* them. For example, if a boy is running to get away from a dog that is chasing him, the dog is the cause of his running and the "getting away" is his purpose. As long as he is still running and the dog is still chasing, he is acting in accordance with his purpose. But only when his running has brought him to safety will his purpose have been met. Of course, if the dog stops running or is diverted, or if the boy suddenly decides the dog might be friendly, everything changes—purpose, cause, behavior.

Those who believe in a God of love whose "work and glory" is to bring about the immortality and eternal life of his children (see Moses 1:39) understand that a divine purpose can govern their lives. Coming to spiritual maturity is a process of coming to understand this purpose and the specific preparations required to meet it. As we have said, the human mind is designed to organize this world. This inherited predisposition serves the purpose of our Creator by driving us to refine over and over again our understanding of the purpose of our lives. The time in which we live requires that we look to a future. During the season of purposes and preparation we are led to examine the purposes of things until we learn a purpose for our life. Then we resolve to prepare to meet whatever we think that purpose is. Attention to spiritual seasons can teach us the ultimate and divine purpose of our lives and show us the preparations necessary to achieve it.

Infants have no concept of passing time, and they sense no purpose in what they do or see. Gradually, the baby and then the child will develop an understanding of cause and effect, and time begins to "flow" as the relationship between events in time is seen and understood.

At an early age, a child's mind will have matured so he can begin to see that certain events will lead to some result. As he matures further, he begins to apply preparations to his purposes. These may be in the thought form of "the teacher will like me if I finish my math first." This purpose, in the form of an idea, influences the child to work rapidly in order to be the first to complete his work. Children without purpose in their minds often do not make adequate preparations and they do not perform as well as they could.

All of this maturing takes place unconsciously. But, gradually purposes come to play an important role in our lives, until, as adults, most of what we do is influenced by our purposes—educational, social, emotional, and religious. We order our lives by what we want to achieve by our preparations. So universal is this process that we could reasonably assume that some distant purpose is at work in the preparation of our minds. The likelihood of this is increased when we recognize that we learn about purposes, and the preparations they require, in stages. Each stage seems to be a foundation for the next.

The Primitive Season

A Pueblo Indian chief once told the noted Swiss psychologist Karl Jung that the sun was kept in its movement across the horizon by the ancient religious ceremonies of his people. According to this chief, if the ceremonies were not performed daily, the sun would eventually stop and all would be in darkness. We can imagine the sense of purpose felt by those who performed the ceremonies and the intricate preparations they would have made. Even though such people have a mistaken notion of cause and effect, they can sustain their sense of purpose because the ceremonies *seem* to prevent the sun from failing in its rounds.

Primitive religious beliefs concerning natural calamities, growth of plants and crops, and unexplained human events have arisen in every human culture as an attempt to make sense out of the unknown. We might explain this universal phenomenon by emphasizing the human fear of the unknown that drives people to contrive beliefs that give them a sense of comfort. This mechanism is seen clearly in young children. When confronted with something beyond their abilities to understand, children come up with simple explanations. If asked, for example, ''What is the thunder?'' a young child might say, ''It is angels going bowling.'' The untutored mind gives a purpose when there is none. But surely this is a step beyond seeing no purpose at all.

The next step, of course, is to come to see the true purposes at work in the world. I see the universal need to explain, to find purpose, as evidence of the divine hand in our creation. This need is created within us all and discovered as we develop through our lives. I believe it is very important for us to know why we are driven to find purposes and to make preparations to achieve them. There are both practical and spiritual benefits.

For one thing, our purposes are the root of our motivations. We are impelled to act when we believe that some desired but unrealized future condition is possible. The more strongly we believe in the imagined event, the more intense will be our preparations; and the better our preparations, the more confident we are of our abilities to achieve our purposes. Parents can more easily motivate children, for example, by helping them think about purposes and what must be done to achieve them. If nothing else, we can observe and ask what children want for themselves. We can even increase their motivation by making the purpose something desirable instead of something fearful. It is not difficult to make our language reflect the potential rewards for their efforts instead of the threat of what will happen if they don't perform.

Having purposes and organizing our lives to prepare for them gives meaning and sense to what we do. Those able to do this are less vulnerable to depression and other unhappy emotions. If we want to live a meaningful life, feeling accomplished, we will spend our existence focused on worthy purposes and our preparations to meet them. There will be, of course, special instances when the recognition of purpose and its required preparation flood into our lives. In such times we can recognize a spiritual season. In such times, life can be dramatically altered. I believe that all humans can recognize such seasons in their lives, and though the experiences are very individual, they all lead suddenly to knowledge of something designed for all who are mortal.

Those who believe in heavenly parents will find little difficulty in understanding how such parents might create a human body designed to help mortals remember them. The universal need to have gods of some kind speaks eloquently that the tendency to worship divine beings is part of us at birth. With no knowledge of anything else, people can create at least gods of wood, metal, or stone which can be seen. What is it that enables mortals to remember an unseen god, believe that he exists, and prepare to meet him? I believe that the propensity for humans to mentally create a purpose and prepare for it allows us to remember and recognize the existence of our God. I like to think that this universal feature of the human mind was carefully and caringly designed by those who loved us enough to wish for our return. It is a wonderful thought that God, knowing our return to him would depend on our ultimate ability to live the kind of life he lives, created a body and mind where all could grow toward a remembrance of him. If we recognize our lifelong development and the significance of our ability to form appropriate purposes and pursue them, we can easily conclude that there is a God who is, though unseen, the kind of being we are becoming.

A Persistent Voice

I have read the biographies and autobiographies of several famous men and women. In most cases, the lives of these people were marked by at least one experience so influential that it affected the rest of their lives. The nature of this experience is interesting and exciting. It usually happens during the middle or late childhood, and the child recognizes that the experience has some special significance. The event comes to be thought of as a way to apply some natural ability possessed by the child. An example of this is when Leonardo da Vinci was taken by his parents to observe an art display. He is reported to have understood how a certain painting was designed and to have suggested what might be done to improve it. This and other similar experiences led his parents to recognize his talent and to provide proper training experiences for him.

Another example is that of Elizabeth Blackwell, one of the first American women doctors. At a young age she found herself captivated by some of her father's work around a hospital. While she was noticing what the nurses and doctors were doing, she found herself fascinated by the doctor's work with his patients. She knew at that moment that she would eventually become a doctor. She had to overcome enormous obstacles put in her way by people who were unprepared to recognize that women could rightfully take a place in the profession of medicine. But she eventually graduated and established one of the first women's hospitals, benefitting the lives of many who came in contact with her.

A modest analysis of these experiences suggests that those who have them often organize their lives from that point and are motivated despite distractions or obstacles to make their life's mission an application of their talent. They acquire a sense of purpose because they come to know about their talents.

I once thought that only those with unusual talents were influenced by this kind of experience. I have found, however, that many people have had a similar significant experience. While probably not universal among humans, this happens enough to warrant our taking note of it. Perhaps many of us can recall an experience that had the effect of directing our focus in a career, in a sense of mission or "calling" in a religious sense, or perhaps in our expression of a unique talent. Often such an experience is comprised of one brief but powerful moment of recognition that will direct an entire life toward a specific purpose. Thereafter, a person's abilities and experiences, the example and instruction of others, will all be channeled into one direction.

Barry Clifford grew up on the coast of Maine. The small towns in the vicinity knew a rich tradition of stories about old sailors, whalers, even pirates. There was a story about one English pirate, Black Sam Bellamy, that was especially rich and colorful. According to this account, the pirate was a merchant by trade who, having failed in business, turned to piracy. He and a partner plundered many ships, eventually capturing a one-hundred-foot brig called *The Whida*. One evening the partners loaded the accumulation of their many raids onto this ship. Then, with all hands drunk, the ship ran into a storm and sank in sight of land. The governor of Massachusetts, wishing to recover the valuables, sent a salvor called Cyprian Southack to salvage the wreck. Southack kept fairly accurate records, writing in detail the description of the exact location of the wreck. He also wrote, ''There have been two hundred men from twenty miles distant plundering the wreck.'' Many readers assumed there was little left of the wreck and its cargo.

As a young boy, Barry Clifford was exposed to this story on many occasions. He remembers clearly that his Uncle Bill, a master storyteller, told him the story at bedtime when he was eight years old. From that time on, the story never faded from his mind. He began to explore the ocean bottom when he was young, and as he grew older his interest deepened. Eventually he spent as much time in the archives reading about these adventurous pirates as he did looking for the ships under water. He felt as though it was his destiny to find *The Whida*.

He started his own business in marine salvage and continued to spend time in libraries, museums, and in any archives that described this one shipwreck. One day his search led him to a different record of Cyprian Southack's report than the one he had seen before. Instead of saying merely that two hundred men plundered the wreck, this report said that, ''there have been two hundred men from twenty miles distant plundering the wreck *of what came ashore.*'' Now, Barry Clifford applied for a license to hunt for treasure and began looking. He found the location described by

Cyprian Southack and began to search for the wreck. He first found an old rudder strap (a piece of metal) which was ridiculed by those who knew of his adventure. He "felt" it was from *The Whida.* Two years later and eighteen feet of sand deeper, gold and silver coins were discovered.

What followed was a discovery of a treasure valued at $400 million. Barry Clifford said, "In the fall of 1982, thirty years after Uncle Bill told me my bedtime story, I sat on the edge of Uncle Bill's bed. This time it was my turn to tell him a pirate's story. He knew I had found her. His eyes sparkled like a child's in anticipation. Uncle Bill died late that night. I am sure he dreamed of treasure." (Story by David White in *Parade,* 27 January 1985.)

If such experiences are common and lead to important worldly purposes, we can easily understand the advantage of special spiritual blessings which inform us of future purposes to prepare for. As in the experience of Barry Clifford, the spiritual knowledge of one's ancestry and abilities is focused toward an unseen future which we cannot see as clearly but which we nevertheless move toward. God apparently believes in purposes and uses them to impel us toward a better preparation for what is to come.

Spiritual Maturity

As we grow, so does the role of purposes in our lives. The beginning is an awareness of the purpose of our actions, then comes the ability to devise purposes and demonstrate the ability to prepare for and achieve them. Next is recognition of special experiences that can lead us to a lifelong purpose that will give direction to our lives. Finally, more experienced and mature, we can understand the last purpose, an understanding which comes in another spiritual season. It is the purpose God has for us—that we should have immortality and eternal life, that we should be like him. And we come to see that, through our faith, all our experiences can turn into preparations for this purpose.

Following the death of my mother, my father and I were riding in the car together when he asked, "Why has this happened to me?" I was not sure how to answer him, and my attempt was inadequate. I have been asked the same question numerous times by others. In truth, I have not been able to find anything of value that could result from some situations: divorce, the abuse of one human by another, and the effects of sin—all have seemed to me totally devoid of any good purpose. Not able to see a purpose, I have sometimes concluded that there was none. I wish I had known enough then to be able to tell my father that my mother's death could have a very important purpose in his life. It was not the design or purpose of someone who wished to leave him alone and uncertain. Rather, he was granted by the natural laws of life an opportunity to exercise his faith and make of this sad event whatever purpose he could create of it. The purpose of Mother's death was whatever Dad chose to make it.

The name of Jehovah was sacred to the early Israelites. In Hebrew it means "the Self-existent One." This name refers to his power to derive his purposes from all that takes place. So much greater than mortals, he is able to make use of an event by turning it into something that promotes his eternal purposes. With surety he can say that man's words and works can pass away, but his will all be fulfilled, regardless of what men do. Satan sought to frustrate the work of God by tempting Adam and Eve, only to discover that his best efforts succeeded in promoting God's eternal purpose of bringing mankind into being. Today the frustration of Satan's designs continues as wars—the product of wicked people—are used by the Lord to spread the gospel or to stimulate research that cures diseases, as personal tragedy brings people closer to spiritual sources, as desolation focuses our minds on the power of the Creator. In small and simple things the worldly wise are confounded, but the weak who humble themselves become strong. The "Self-existent One" turns every event toward the accomplishment of his purpose; and by recognizing the spiritual seasons that give us the opportunity, we can become like him in this.

When I was fifteen, my two brothers and one of my sisters were all on missions for the Church at the same time. My father prepared our family farm to provide the extra income to support three missionaries. He expanded his small dairy herd by buying some purebred Wisconsin heifers, which were reputed to be excellent at producing milk. Dad also rented some additional land in order to increase his crop production.

I was the only son remaining, and Dad let me know that it was going to be up to the two of us. We planted that spring with the hope found in every farming family. Those new heifers began freshening in the spring and summer, adding to the size of the dairy herd and to the monthly milk income. We worked hard, and the sugar beets, grain, potatoes, and alfalfa looked beautiful that summer.

We looked forward to the weekly letters coming from Australia, England, and Chicago. We learned the names of companions, cities, and investigators. People in our town asked about the missionaries, and altogether we felt a sense of blessing and accomplishment for what we were doing.

There were many days when we worked in the fields from sunrise to late at night. Mother always seemed to have the meals ready whenever we arrived home. On many occasions, she was the only one waiting, and as we sat and talked at the table, I learned many useful and memorable things. I do not know how my parents were able to keep up the pace. They both seemed to put two days into one. My two sisters who were at home spent numerous hours driving tractors and hay trucks. We all were fueled by the idea that we were part of a great work and we were important.

At the end of the summer all looked satisfactory, and we awaited the harvest with the anticipation of meeting all the obligations and supporting those missionaries. Sometimes during a lull in the work or when Dad and I were driving to a field, the urge to look more closely would overcome us. Looking at the straight rows and thick crops from the road was not enough. With some unspoken agreement, the one driving would stop and we would climb out of the old pickup truck, and walk to the fields just to look, touch, and sometimes taste. Dad almost always grabbed a stalk of wheat, pulled a potato plant, or tore off a beet leaf, and brought it back to the truck. Then, assured that all was well, we would take these small monuments to our hopes and drive off to our work.

There were many such experiences that summer. Some of them were the ordinary part of a fifteen-year-old's growing. Early one morning in late summer, I went to start the irrigation water on a field of potatoes. The plants had grown large and had "crossed the rows" so all the eye could see was an ocean of green dimpled by small white blossoms. The sun had not yet risen, and I worked as much to get warm as to get the right amount of water down each row. As I neared the completion of my task, the sun shone down from the foothills from the east across the valley in which we lived, casting the long and lovely shadows of the morning.

As I stood leaning and resting on my shovel, I was transfixed by what I saw. I thought, "Look what I have done. I have prepared the earth, planted the seeds, cultivated, and watered. I have created something beautiful." As I stood there watching, feeling humbly proud of myself, I heard the water trickle in the rows, felt the warmth of the sun, and heard a voice within me say, "This is God's creation, and you are his, too." I felt a rush of feeling that was part apology and part gratitude, and I wished that I could grasp the earth in my arms and embrace it. I was being taught what God was to man, and I have not forgotten that lesson.

School started and the routine of hard work changed. One afternoon I came home and prepared to take some fuel for the tractor to the field where Dad was working. As I drove past the corral where the fresh heifers and cows were penned, I noticed that two had calved. But something was wrong with the calves. They were obviously premature. When I told Dad, a worried look crossed his face, but he said nothing. The next day the veterinarian told Dad that his herd was affected by brucellosis, and all the animals that had it would have to be destroyed. Apparently one of the new heifers had not been correctly inoculated and had brought it to Dad's herd.

I stood on the railing of the fence and watched quietly as one animal after another was tested and each one with the disease had a red tag punched in its ear. In ten days a herd of forty or more animals was reduced to sixteen. The diseased animals were sold to an animal products firm for seventy-five dollars apiece.

There were some somber moments at our dinner table that fall, but the demands to get ready for the harvest occupied us. One day after we began to harvest the sugar beets, it snowed a deep, water-heavy, lovely snow. The fields were soaked and muddy. As a result, the harvest was stopped. Dad arranged to get extra tires for the tractors, hoping they would not sink. Then we waited. Days came and went with as little warmth in them as was found in my parents' faces. The weather stayed that way all fall until all the beets and most of the potatoes were ruined.

Mother kept writing encouraging letters to the missionaries, and Dad did what he could with the animals. One Saturday morning we were walking toward the corrals to do the feeding. Dad stopped and looked across the snow-covered field where the harvester sat in a true poverty of sound. I knew he was alone in his thoughts and did not ask anything. After a few moments he stopped his reverie and said simply, ''At least I won't have to ride the tractor in the cold.'' That was all he ever said about it. There was no depression, no acrimonious anger toward God, no envy of those more favored by the weather. We found ways to support the missionaries by selling a steer or two, scrimping, and going without.

Dad planted again in the spring. He never lost another crop to the weather again—except one year when I was serving my mission. Dad said he was glad I was the last of his children to go.

My parents could have been resentful, could have doubted God's love for or interest in them. Instead, they turned their experience into increased faith and solid devotion to the Lord. They both became more like him by making a season beyond their control serve the purposes they selected. Like the "Self-existent One," they turned a challenge into a spiritual accomplishment. Their children believe both will feel comfortable in his presence.

All will face some seasons that may not seem to have good purpose in them. We can become more like the Savior of the world when we are willing to create our own purposes from such times. Those who are mature enough to apply the principle of faith and make their purpose one that is acceptable to God will be better prepared to meet him on that final day.

Chapter 4

THRESHOLDS

He was tall, dark, and handsome, and coeds at our college were very creative in their attempts to attract his attention. He was in his late twenties, a returned missionary, and very eligible. He dated quite often, but nothing definite ever seemed to come of it. After every breakup, he was increasingly frustrated. He wanted to get married, and he was afraid he was never going to make it. I met him after one of his several breakups. His disappointment was obvious, but I was unprepared when he said, "I think they [the girls] are interested in me only for my looks." Smiling, I told him that that is usually a girl's lament. "Yes, but they don't seem really interested in *me*," he replied.

We talked more, and he admitted that several times he had been the one to back away when a relationship had approached the time of decision. He saw that part of his problem was an unwillingness to decide and to commit even when he had found an appropriate girl. We concluded that he needed to continue dating.

After this conversation, we did not communicate for quite a while. Then one day he called, telling me he had been dating a girl he liked and had reached the point where a decision should be made. I was inexperienced and unsure of exactly what to do to help a person make as important a decision as marriage, but I invited him to talk again. He told me of her many fine qualities, including her beauty, testimony, domestic skills, and the fact that she seemed to like him. "With all this," I asked, "why can't you decide?" "I don't know," was the answer. "I'm afraid of being wrong, or of meeting a girl I'll like better. And I'm not sure that I trust myself." "Yet, you don't like being single?" I questioned. "I hate it," he said. "I want to be married, but I'm just not sure I can do it."

I told him that all good decisions are made from good information, and if he was not able to decide now, it might be because he did not have the right information. I proposed that he needed to know more about himself when he was with this girl rather than just about her. Together we selected ten things he would do with or for her in succession. After each, he would evaluate his feelings. If he felt good, he would go on to the next step until he had reached the tenth, which was an actual proposal of marriage. The first thing was to send her flowers. I suggested he make the arrangements for this in front of me, because the look on his face made me think he might do nothing. After he phoned the florist from my office, he smiled and reported that he felt good enough to go on to step two.

A couple of days passed and he phoned saying that I had gotten him into real trouble. I did not realize his comment was tongue-in-cheek and with some concern asked, "What happened?" "She accepted," he said. "Now we're getting married." He told me he had followed our agreement and had taken all nine steps and felt very happy and satisfied after each one. He felt so sure of his feelings that he took her one evening to the Provo Temple grounds with the intent of taking step ten. After they talked awhile, he asked for her hand in marriage. "I had been concentrating on my own feelings so much that I forgot to worry about her answer, and just for a few seconds I was afraid she would say no. But she said yes, and now I'm more afraid. What do I do now?" "The next two things," I replied. He has done that and more, having formed a happy marriage with her and created a lovely family.

I remember him with a bit of humor mixed with affection. He was faced with a decision that only he could make. He was free to make it, but afraid to do so. It was one of his thresholds, and he had finally been able to cross it.

Like my friend, all of us face personal thresholds which make us realize that living requires choosing. Our development toward some better state results from choosing properly. The seasons of thresholds are opportunities for growth or stagnation. The choices are ours to make with more freedom than we often accept.

Thresholds of Personal Freedom

We live in a society designed to vigorously protect by law certain basic freedoms. These freedoms (e.g., the right to assemble, worship, speak peacefully according to our own consciences) are very important to us and deserve our attention and careful concern. But there is another type of freedom that is not within the power of law to provide or restrict. This is personal freedom to choose from available alternatives. How this freedom is exercised determines whether or not life is happy.

There are some seasons of life when the issue of personal freedom is especially paramount. These are the moments when we commit ourselves to paths that, once taken, prevent us from choosing other parallel paths. These moments are the thresholds that take us into the uncertainties of the future and all that we will find in life. Within the space of a few years, most people are called upon to cross the thresholds of mature commitment to a religion, a mate, a career, and a place to live. These choices are made by most people, most of the time, with a modest amount of strain. For some, however, any of them can create major problems.

We learn some things about freedom when we face these decisions. First, we are not free to accept or reject freedom. It is ours by nature. Anything we do, including doing nothing, is an exercise in freedom. Second, all our choices, even those that are most ''informed,'' are made without full knowledge of the future. In some cases, we will find later that we would not have chosen as we did if we had known more.

Adolescence is an important time for thresholds. It is a natural time for choosing new paths, as the child grows from dependency on parents and family to the independence of physical maturity. Thus, the flow of human society goes on. Those who fail to make these choices at the time dictated by cultural expectations (tempered as necessary by the Lord's guidance on the matter) will find the choices increasingly difficult because of fears that they somehow are not adequate, and because they acquire knowledge which makes the decisions more complex. The longer choices are postponed past this expected time, the less likely it is that they ever will be made.

A decision to cross an emotional or psychological threshold is like deciding to leave the warm and protective interior of a home. With a small step we are through the door and away finding a less certain world. Parents and older children who say good-bye in airports, on front porches, or in bus depots know the feelings of the threshold. The sadness at parting is mixed with hope at the potential and apprehension about the uncertainties of the future. As with all seasons that try the spirit, this is a time for faith.

All of us will find thresholds, created by time and circumstance, that will require us to summon inner reserves of faith to launch ourselves unalterably toward some destination. Failing to make the crossing in such a season can result in a lifetime of bitter disappointment in ourselves.

At such a time the choice may not seem clear. Is it better to cross and go ahead or remain as we are? Some spirit tells us that staying will diminish our growth, and so we move toward the door. But the closer we get to it, the more we fear and wish to retreat. "Someone help me," is the inner cry, and we shrink. Some of us want an Eternal Father to decide because he knows the future and can guarantee success. Sometimes he whispers the course we should take, but more often he only reassures us of his love and leaves us to learn from the exercise of our freedom, leaves us to grow spiritually as we cross the smaller thresholds in preparation for the greater.

Integrity and Love

When we are very young, we cannot hide much of what we feel from the view of others. Transparently, our actions show what we think and feel to anyone who cares to look. As we grow older, however, we learn we can lie if we wish to, or keep things within us that others cannot see. Pretense is possible. The perceived need for this is exaggerated when children become adolescents and are faced with pressures to be approved of by others. Teenage bodies change and powerful self-consciousness increases. It is a time when making impressions, seeming to be what others will accept, becomes very important.

Nearly all of us face this circumstance. Most make our way through it to adulthood and a mature sense of integrity. Some, however, retain the desire for approval, allowing it to pervert their souls. This is what happened to a man who has become one of my friends.

In addition to the usual discomforts, this man was burdened in adolescence by having a famous father to whom he was invariably compared. "You look just like him," it was often said. "You're Tommy Anderson's boy, aren't you?" they would say. Tommy Anderson (the name is fictitious) was a great athlete. Everyone thought his son Tommy, Jr., would be like him. His son, my friend, wanted to be like his dad; especially he wanted to have the same kind of recognition. Unfortunately, he was not quite as talented as his father, and he was placed in a situation where he was faced with a choice between making excuses for a poor performance or accepting failure in front of a great many people. In the small town where he lived it seemed to him intolerable to fail, both for his and his dad's sake. He gave excuses. People were more than willing to accept what he said. After all, he was Tommy Anderson's son.

This experience was an effective teacher. He became an easy talker who bluffed his way through classes at school. He impressed girl- and boyfriends, and was even able to hide the truth from his parents. In order to be approved of by others, he had only to say impressive things, and if he could not measure up to all his promises, he could, with great facility, shift the responsibility elsewhere. He became the perfect machine. His good looks, easy-talking style, and friendly ways were impressive indeed; but most important, he could instantly learn what others wanted to hear and what would impress them, and he could and would say it. He was a creature devoted to the value of image making. His devotion, however, made him a stranger to himself, for he hid the truth even from himself in order to look good. Unfortunately, he was at the age when children establish an identity for life.

After he left school, he found a natural place in sales and gradually rose to a high position in his company. He married and became the father of five children. He and his wife were seldom emotionally close, and he was usually uninvolved with his children.

Approval-seeking and the dishonesty this requires is based on anxiety. That is why the first impulse is to make the good impression. Anxious people require occasional "fixes" to temporarily calm them, and he was no different. He sought out occasions for attention, including praise and adoration. This initially took the form of aspiring to church and civic positions. With each new recognition, he felt justified that he was all right. But one day, in his travels as a salesman, he met a woman who appeared unusually impressed with him. He was flattered and pursued her. To see if she was attracted enough, he proposed they spend the evening together. She accepted. He had found another way to obtain approval. He doesn't clearly remember that night or the nights with other women that followed. He was addicted to the shallowest flattery and the weakest approval, all the time thinking he was significant and manly. He failed to recognize that he was as controlled and manipulated as the women he used.

Publicly he was well thought of and mostly respected. He was unable to tell the truth about himself, for by now he did not know what he thought or believed.

As is true for most people like this, he could not keep everything hidden forever, and eventually he was found out. His wife asked him to leave home. He began to drink excessively and to fail in his work. Because of this, he sought professional help. He benefitted little until, as requested, he began writing a personal journal. One day, after reading what he had written earlier, he discovered he had lied when writing in his own journal. This realization helped him understand that he was not able to tell the truth even to himself.

When it came time to tell the truth to others, however, he was so frightened that he could not do it. His old facade took over and he again spun a web of dishonesty. Though he now had a greater understanding of what he was doing, he was still fearful of telling the truth, of admitting responsibility, and of concerning himself more with his standards than with what others thought. Every time he tried to tell the truth, he expected rejection. People could not understand what he was doing. He would start to speak, scrutinize their faces, and if he saw disapproval, he would change from the truth to something else in midsentence. Aware of himself now, he felt increasingly embarrassed for the way he was. He relived many of his hypocritical moments and felt ashamed. He knew that to shake the guilt he would have to tell the truth, but to do it meant risking what he feared most.

He stayed this way for a few weeks, trying to get the strength to cross the threshold from the certainty of habitual deceit into the uncertainty integrity would bring him. Back and forth he wavered. To someone practiced in truth-telling, his challenge would have looked insignificant. But lying was his way of life, and he was terrified. He prayed more often and more fervently. And then one day (I knew because he was calm), he crossed the threshold, and his sense of integrity became more important than the approval of others.

Crossing the threshold created spiritual growth for my friend. He had lied to so many people in so many different places, that he knew it would take him months to tell the truth to everyone. But he did it. He became better and better at it and began to restore his life. He was less afraid and less susceptible to temptation.

It was at this point that he realized he had never had a deep, loving relationship with anyone, including his wife and children. Then he learned that honesty is the root of genuine love. One who has tried to find security through deception will create a social image perhaps but will be unable to love deeply. Even when we know that honesty is better, there still is fear. When the truth is more important than what we want others to think, then we can approach others with confidence and feel the touching of souls we call love.

"I Can't Go On"

Some thresholds appear in our lives unexpected and unwelcome. Arising from events we never wanted to happen, they invite us to growth we are not prepared to make. The future is frightening at these times, and we feel small. So incapable do we feel that we mope and cry. When we are finally exhausted by this, we resent, then we hate. Something unseen and terrible seems to have forced this to happen. Testimonies waver, cynicism becomes the companion of self-doubt, and we say to ourselves "I cannot go on." The choice is to retreat into useless self-pity or to push ourselves out of the door, across the threshold we never planned to cross, and on into a future we must make by ourselves. It can be a terrible season, but those who conquer it wear the laurels of the truly valiant. They go on a day at a time and find that life can be rewarding still.

We face secret trials of temptation, bondage to small habits known only to us, or an unexpected challenge found in a position we thought safe. We call these seasons by such names as divorce, financial failure, broken hearts, loneliness, death of a loved one. They are times when life is difficult because a crisis of pain creates a forbidding future.

Such is the case of a woman whose life was marred by such a torrent of misery that it could hardly be believed. I was an eye-witness to most of it, and so I know that what I tell truly happened. Her sadness began, as with so many others, in her childhood. Her father, a cold and sometimes mean-spirited man, married a fearful and aloof woman. Together they tried to form a family where the emotional bonds of love and affection were less constant than the nothingness of neglect and the hurt of abuse. They lived in a small town in Utah where growing up was made a bit more bearable for their daughter by the constancy of friends and traditions.

After high school, she met and married a handsome but timid man, and they set up housekeeping near her parents' home. From the first, their marriage was punctuated by anger and insecurity. Motivated by a belief that life would improve, they prospered some and had three children. Marital conflict intensified as the pressures they faced increased. Neither was able to calmly take care of their children, so they left them to the TV or let them run loose. Their marriage ended when he announced that he preferred a homosexual life.

The next few months were filled with trials over custody of the sons. Most of their possessions had to be sold to pay lawyers' fees. She grew increasingly embittered at him and at life. She slept for most of each day, barely preparing one, or at most two meals. One day, at a friend's invitation, she went to a bar that specialized in serving "lonely hearts." There she met a man who proposed a night of drink and passion. She accepted both. The thrills seemed to be a cure for her desperate life, and she began to frequent the bar, going through a series of nameless and faceless men and unmemorable drinks.

The resulting neglect of her children was finally noticed by the school authorities. Their inquiries caused her to reflect about her life-style, and she decided to change. By this time, she had to accept state welfare. All went well for a few weeks until she went with her friend for one last night to the bar. She became intoxicated and was taken home by a strange man. Too drunk to resist, she was forced to allow sexual intercourse. At first she thought that the only reminder of that evening was a case of genital herpes. She soon found, however, that she was pregnant.

Single, mother of three children, poverty-stricken, and distressed, she sought help from the Church. The local leaders were kind and offered much help. She confessed her transgressions, and in a few weeks Church membership was withdrawn from her. Instead of feeling rejected, she felt relieved to be on her way back. As her pregnancy progressed, her spirits improved. At this point her former husband, having heard of her pregnancy, decided to seek custody of the children.

I traveled to a nearby city to testify in her behalf at the custody hearing. I will never forget the scene we saw then: a woman who feared the loss of her children because she was unable to hide the evidence her former husband wanted to use against her. But the judge did not hear the case that day, and her former husband apparently lost interest in pursuing the matter. When it was time for the child's birth, she asked if I could be with her at the hospital because her parents refused, as did her brothers and sisters. Her delivery was hard and, with her resistance lowered, she came close to a serious nervous breakdown. Sedated, she finally slept. She awakened in two days to begin care of her new son.

Finally, a brother came for her and the children. She lived with his family until she became stronger and then moved into a nearby vacant house. The events of her life were marked by financial struggles, stress with the children, and anxiety so great that it easily crippled her efforts to prosper. I lost track of the number of times she quit and then started again. Her phone calls began with a trembling voice. She wept many tears and often said, "I can't go on. What am I going to do?" She finally found work and took herself off welfare by selling her piano—her last possession— in order to repay some overpayment by the welfare services. She was rebaptized into the Church.

In situations of this kind, those who try to help are confronted with feelings of helplessness and futility. There is only so much one person can do to help another. Knowing of someone's pain and not being able to assuage it is among life's most difficult experiences. At last I could only remind her of the Savior, who told us to place our burdens on him. "Will he feed my children?" she cynically asked. "He might feed you," I answered. She began to study the scriptures and to pray.

By this time, her oldest child was twelve years old. He had often tried to let her know of her inadequate parenting by misbehaving, but now he refined his anger and made time at home unbearable. He claimed he wished to go and be with his father who was then living with his male lover. His mother could not find any other help and in real desperation agreed. I cannot forget the expression on her face when we discussed whether I thought her former husband would educate the son in his ways. After the boy left, she stayed in bed weeping for two or three days.

A few months later she learned of work in the town where her mother lived. She decided to move there, mostly to see if she could mend her broken relationship with her mother. Her parents had divorced, and lately her mother seemed to be more pleasant.

Arriving in the town, she found a home and began work. It seemed too difficult to go to church or civic activities or even to be with anyone except one or two close friends; so she introduced more loneliness into her life. The relationship with her mother was a bit better, with fewer disagreements and more affection. She said once that she finally had to say, "Mother, I want to come over and I just want you to love me." Through her efforts, her mother finally began to soothe the ache of emptiness which the daughter had felt for years.

In a grocery store one day, she met a man who seemed quite interesting and interested in her. Affection grew while they dated and, feeling safe, she began reciprocating his physical affection. After having gone further than she should have, she learned he was married. Her response was a profound depression that left only when panic was present. She could not sleep, her appetite left, and she had uncontrolled crying binges which left her exhausted. She could barely get to work, and she could not care for her children at all. They let her know about it in the way children do, and things grew worse. I received another phone call and through the crying knew immediately who was there. "I can't go on," the voice said. "I can't sleep, eat, or walk." By this time we had discovered her sense of humor, and I told her I was glad to hear from her because thus far my day had not had any sincere misery. She became so incapable that to help her sons she sent the second and third in the path of their older brother—to live with their father. She spent the next few days weeping in bed.

She gradually gained strength by forcing herself to exercise, to talk with people, and to establish a routine which she followed. She needed to be with people, and I asked again of her feelings about her religion. In a moment of candor, she told of her fear to rely on anything. Her parents had failed her. Her husband had betrayed her. Some man had assaulted her. God had not seemed to help much. "I will try to pray again," she offered.

It did not occur to me then that she was in her mental house of unhappiness and feared crossing the threshold to faith. Believing, hoping, relying on someone was frightening, and she shrank from doing it. One day she visited her bishop, who kindly invited her to come to church. "With all I've done?" she wondered. She went, joined the choir, and was asked to give a talk. Her scripture studies began in earnest. She became calmer and more secure, and her warmth and vitality reappeared. Faith was becoming as real to her as money or her car—and more important. It is easy to talk of faith when we have not known suffering. But for one who had known little else, believing in a loving Heavenly Father was difficult.

Her next concern was the loss of her children. She telephoned them, and her oldest son would not talk to her. She invited them for Christmas, and the two youngest came but the oldest would not. She saved the price of a plane ticket and prepared to go to him for a visit. She was frightened about what she would find there. Finally she was able to talk to her oldest son, then nineteen, on the telephone. After arranging schedules so he could pick her up at the airport, he said, "Mother, I don't want you to preach to me. Will you come and just love me?" She knew exactly what to do.

The Thought Before We Act

All of us have known or will know the season of thresholds. Because they are common to all of us we can understand their effects on us. Sometimes we attend to the dramatic parts of our choices and think only of our alternatives. But we need also to recognize the gift we are given to exercise conscious thought before we act and the spiritual maturity that comes when we recognize this gift and learn to use it. When we think about how we think, we can improve the quality of our choices.

I discovered as a growing man that I began making decisions by assuming there were only two possible alternatives. Some of my selections did not turn out well, and I was frequently discouraged. One day, thinking about how I had thought about things, I discovered my assumption. Thereafter, I tried to look for more than two alternatives and usually found some better than those I started with. The quality of my decisions improved. I have known many others who, because of failure to think about how they decide, choose unwisely.

The importance of reflecting about our method of making choices will be shown in the pattern of our lives. Those who create a mature and wise style of choosing will grow from the freedom of it and also from their correct choices. Spiritual maturity stems from deliberation and thoughtfulness so that when we do act, even righteously, it is because of our freedom and not from some hidden impulse we are unaware of. We must know, and know that we know, the truth.

The thresholds we cross are seasons of spiritual growth. They increase our sense of freedom and control over the future. Feeling more free, we can assume greater amounts of responsibility and come closer to finding eternal life.

Chapter 5

COMMITMENTS

During the span of life, we each have an opportunity to do many different things. Depending on our resources, we can try one or more careers, travel to many places, acquire knowledge, select or change a religious affiliation, and live in one place or move to many different locations. Besides resources, the only limitations on our choices are time and desire. If we spend little time with any one choice and go from one thing to another, we will increase the variety of things we can do. If we narrow our choices and do things for a longer period of time, we will be able to do fewer. We cannot do everything, though some may have the illusion that this is possible. We all will, of necessity, value some things more than others. When we honor what we place in highest value, we establish a commitment. This is a long-term attachment wherein we channel our lives and form enduring involvements.

Some people avoid long-term commitments because they do not want to narrow their choices; they think something better may appear later if they are free from previous commitment, or they think that life is more exciting if there is greater variety to it. These people could tell us to what extent variety brings happiness. But only those who form and honor commitments can tell us whether or not commitment is better. Only people who have lived lives filled with devotion can, at the end of life, tell if such a life was worth it. All are faced with times when commitments can be made. These are spiritual seasons that can begin our education in endurance and honor.

What we learn in life as well as what we achieve is to a great degree determined by our commitments. The path to eternal life is called "narrow," for example, because all who take it are required to commit to it as a destiny and to give up choices that conflict with it. It is called "strait" because those who follow it to the end must repeatedly avoid attractive distractions found by the wayside. Any movement toward the correct destination and away from a distracting route is verified by a spiritual sensation. This spiritual season can be as brief as a momentary choice to stay on the path, or it can be a collection of validating feelings that what we have been doing (are doing, will do) is right.

This spiritual guidance along the straight and narrow path will teach us that some of what we do in life does not require that we make enduring commitments. We may change jobs, move from one place to another, try a variety of schools, change hobbies, or rotate clothing styles. But some parts of life are lived correctly only in continued devotion to commitments. Evidence that most people understand this is seen in the general instinctive appreciation for anyone who has lived a life of commitment to what he believed was right. We seem to know how easy it is to be inconsistent, and when some endure we respect them and take hope for ourselves.

Enduring marriages, lifelong friendships, years of faithful service in the Church or community, examples of devoted parenthood or dedicated teaching are among those evidences of commitment we seem to admire instinctively. If we evaluate the commitments we honor most, we will find that they all have to do with the care and development of human beings. I can still remember my mother's stories about people who overcame obstacles in order to develop a talent, conquer a handicap, or live a life of charity towards others. The human race seems possessed of a natural desire to preserve itself, and we naturally honor those who make the most useful contributions to this effort. I think there is a spiritual motivation behind this desire.

Even the animal kingdom exhibits this desire in some measure. Many advanced species of animal life use selection processes that in effect determine which individuals will be permitted to procreate and extend genetic life for the species. Male white-tailed deer, for example, engage during the mating season in contests of endurance and strength that determine which ones will sire the next generation. As a result, the tendency is for the strongest animals to add their characteristics to the species, preventing the weaker and the unfit from doing so. This helps to protect the species.

It would not be hard to imagine divine beings, former humans, who have a plan to determine who will be allowed to propagate their species. Our selection process is probably not physical, but it would include the way we care for one another, honor our commitments to our spouses, and nurture the growth of our children. These tasks, of course, require a lifetime of commitment to correct behavior and will, I believe, comprise much of the basis for selecting those who will be permitted to propagate spirit children in the eternities ahead.

It is in our seasons of commitment that responsibility and endurance are learned. Of necessity, all will commit to something. Our spiritual seasons also help us know which commitments have the greatest worth.

Our Spiritual Inheritance

Sometimes we can understand ourselves better by observing correspondence in nature that calls to mind a human trait. This is one way we can discover the spiritual motivation for making and keeping lasting commitments.

In the home of a neighbor one evening, I was enjoying a conversation about things we had always wanted to do but had never done. I told my friend that from the time I was a boy I had wanted to travel through Alaska and go salmon fishing. His response surprised me. He matter-of-factly said, "Let's go." In time, distance, and money such a trip seemed a remote possibility to me, so I did not pay a great deal of attention to him. Two or three days later he called to say that the arrangements had been made, and we would be leaving in July, three months away. I did not know at the time we first talked that a few years earlier he had worked in the Alaska State Attorney General's office and was well acquainted with the people and the area. So we went.

When we arrived, I was truly awed by the spectacular beauty of Alaska. And because they were plentiful, I was even able to catch some salmon. Prior to our return flight, my friend drove our group to an inland river where we were able to see salmon in the spawning place, repeating a round of creation that had, I suppose, been going on for centuries.

As I stood and watched these fish, I felt deep stirrings. It seemed to me quite miraculous that salmon could leave their spawning grounds, travel a great distance, and then return to the exact place where they had hatched. That they were the same fish and not strangers had been established earlier by biologists who traced the salmon's migrations by using small radio transmitters planted in them before they left the spawning area.

At the University of Washington in Seattle scientists built an artificial canal connecting waters of Puget Sound and the hatcheries in their laboratories. Eggs were artificially fertilized, and when they hatched, the fingerlings were protected as they grew. Then the young salmon, some with transmitters embedded under their skins, were released down the artificial canal to begin their journey into the ocean. During the next two to three years scientists tracked the travels of the salmon out into the North Pacific feeding grounds. And, at the end of the three-year cycle, grown salmon swam into the canal and returned to their origin.

Having established that the same salmon returned to their hatching place, the scientists were interested in answering another question. They wanted to know how the individual fish could locate and return to a specific place among thousands of rivers and streams along the Pacific coast. Their research led them to discover cells near the surface of the salmon's skin that are extraordinarily sensitive to light and water temperature. At the time of hatching, these cells learn or record the light and water temperature at their location. These cells lie dormant until the fish reach maturity and can spawn or fertilize eggs themselves. When this time is reached, the dormant cells become active and create a sensation of discomfort. Impelled to end the discomfort, the fish begin their amazing migration. They come from their feeding grounds in the North Pacific and travel inland, in some cases up rivers for several hundred miles. All travel with increasing intensity in their attempts to return. That any do return is a magnificent accomplishment. They are a true monument to all living.

As I stood looking at the fish who had spawned and were about to die, I knew these were they who had lived long enough to successfully participate in creating the next generation. I fell into an absorbed meditation that lasted well into the plane ride home. Perhaps it was the beauty of the place, the newness of it for me, or the pleasant company of my friends that caused my reflection. Regardless, I have clear memories of that time, a time when I knew that I was in a river of time going forward to return to my origin.

Several years later, I was reading an article about migratory birds. The author reported studies that sought to determine how these birds were able to locate a fairly specific place, though having to fly thousands of miles. One species, I read, migrated from the Arctic Circle to Antarctica and back each year. The birds hatched in the Arctic were able to find the nesting grounds of their species in the Antarctic even though they had never been there. It was assumed this was possible because the younger birds simply accompany the older. Some scientists caught a few of these young birds, tagged them, and drove them more than 500 miles out of the usual migratory route, before releasing them. Most of these birds, without the companionship and direction of older birds, found their nesting grounds even though they had never previously seen them.

These scientists, like the ones studying the salmon, were interested in learning how such a journey was possible. They discovered cells just beneath the bird's skulls that were sensitive to magnetic attraction. They now believe that the birds fly to the location that satisfies the impulses of these cells. There is a clear signal from within that indicates movement toward the desired destination and causes discomfort if they are off course. These birds, in other words, have inherited the means of finding their way.

It seemed clear to me that human beings who journey through mortality could also have an inherited way of telling if they are on or off course. I could see how those who designed our bodies could equip them with a means of guiding us back to where we came from. Latter-day Saints are taught about the Light of Christ which is born into every person. This light signals what is true and not true. It is a subtle inner feeling of comfort if the direction is sure, and feeling of discomfort if it is not. At the moment we act or are about to act, a signal is given. At that very moment, we can respond to the sensation of rightness within, or disregard it in favor of some distraction. How we respond will determine whether or not we can devote our lives to our commitments. The ability to commit oneself is the mark of the spiritually advanced and is rewarded by the increased experience of spiritual things.

Our Eternal Commitment

Crossing the thresholds of adolescence brings us to a time when most desire to form a stable attachment to a member of the opposite sex. No one knows for certain whether the desire is from a "cultural expectation" that we marry or from a sense of readiness caused by loneliness. Most feel the yearning and enter courtship to satisfy it. Through our search, we try to find "the right one," the one who satisfies the inner sense of what is correct. We date, evaluate, and learn. Finally, when we have refined our sense of what is best for us, we are ready. Some acquire a readiness and do not have a chance to join themselves to another. Others marry before they are ready and risk commitment they may not be able to make permanent. Marriage, for those who are ready, is the single most consuming commitment begun and maintained throughout life.

The place of marriage in our eternal scheme of things is so important that it deserves a lifetime of devotion to it. Spiritual growth is, therefore, inextricably tied to our marriages and whether or not we make them succeed. Those willing to live spiritually and be guided by truth will find the greater happiness. This is because spiritually-minded people usually understand the importance of love, patience, and unselfishness, which are necessary to maintain the bond of commitment.

When we marry, a ceremony is only the beginning of what the commitment is to become. But if we begin believing that our agreement with each other will last eternally, we have declared our intent to develop a commitment that will match the beauty of this idea. To hold to this commitment, we must sacrifice many other possibilities in order to develop the finest qualities within us. Otherwise, we will settle for a mechanical marriage or will, eventually, not have one at all.

When we marry, we are confronted first by the need to separate emotionally from our families of origin and from friends in order to strengthen the marriage. It is often not easy to do. For families, emotional ties formed over many years are involved and both parents and married children must let go. As married couples we learn when and how much to put time alone together ahead of time with the families we grew up in. We must learn to recognize which of our feelings toward each other stem from our family experiences and not from each other. Then we must develop acts of commitment to show each other that the marriage relationship is primary. When we marry, we promise to spend the rest of our lives and beyond exercising our will to be committed and our faith that the commitment will bring us happiness.

One young husband described his wrestle with this responsibility. "When I married," he said, "I truly believed that I loved my wife and would always be loyal to her." For the first years of their marriage he was in school. They were not able to spend very much time together due to demands of school, work, and church. Even when their children came, they were worked into an already busy schedule. He said they never argued very much, partly because they did not have time, but at the end of four years both of them found themselves becoming increasingly unhappy. He began to worry that he had married the wrong person, and his unhappiness became depression. One day, after a minor disagreement with his wife, he went off to school and work. At the end of the day he was still unhappy. Instead of going home, he told how, overcome with sadness, he lay in the front seat of his car and wept. He said, "I couldn't think of many good things about my wife or my marriage."

He told of thinking about a divorce and feeling justified in doing so because of what he thought was her mistreatment of him. "But then there were our two children," he said, "what my parents would think, and my commitment to the teachings of the Church. At the same time, though, I was quite miserable."

For some reason, then unknown to him, he heard a voice ask this question. "Would you rather die having honored your commitment, or knowing there was a wife and children somewhere that you left?" "I knew," he said, "that despite my present unhappiness, I wanted to be the type of person who honored his agreements. I had seen what divorce does to some families, and I didn't like that." Then the voice said again, "Then you cannot always think you married the wrong person when there is unhappiness. You must commit yourself and be loyal to her."

"I went home that night," the young man said, "resolved to be faithful in my thoughts and acts." He was able to rearrange his schedule a little to spend more time with his wife. "I tried to work at solving our differences instead of thinking about having made a bad decision. I soon realized that most of my unhappiness was due to my lack of commitment, not to problems in my marriage as I had thought. My renewed interest helped her, and we both adjusted to make us more satisfied."

His experience is not unlike that of many others. Whether or not we commit to our eternal partner and avoid distractions is a matter of faith that a life of devotion is better than what seem to be attractive alternatives. We do it first because we believe it to be true. But we find to our happy surprise that emotions develop into a firm spiritual bond that indeed will last forever. The power we gain by honoring this commitment will give us marriages which last and, now or then, children to bring joy.

Knowing Our Destiny

There is a reason that it is important to learn how to commit to a person, a cause, or an ideal. Through our commitments we can exert some control over the events that will take place in the future. College students who are distracted too much, for example, find themselves unable to pass classes and may fail. For most, it is not the lack of intelligence but the inability to commit to regular study that makes it impossible to graduate. It is useful to recall the story of the man listening to the great pianist. After the concert, the man was introduced to the renowned artist, to whom he said, "I would give half my life to be able to play that well." The great pianist said quietly in reply, "That is just what I have given."

We can see what this idea may mean about our spiritual lives. When we can control ourselves and carry out our commitments to do and be good, then we earn an eternal destiny. Living true to eternal ideals must be a basis for our development toward exaltation. Yet we often do not think of this ability as a spiritual gift and something that some are better at than others, though that is true at the time of birth and as a result of what we learn or fail to learn during mortality. Starting something worthwhile and continuing until it is completed requires that we accept guidance and motivation from the Spirit of Truth.

I first learned about what commitments do for us and others early in my teens. Each spring, after they had delivered their calves, my father's cows were combined with my uncle's cattle and trailed to the summer ranch. The trip usually took three to four days, and all aspiring cowboys looked forward to it with great anticipation. Sometimes there would be two or three other herds on the same road, and the parade was enough to thrill any country boy.

I remember the year I first learned about the two red cows. As the cattle grew accustomed to the walking, a pace was set that was usually kept for most of the trip. The young calves were at the rear of the herd, followed by a truck that would pick them up if they could not keep up. The cows and bulls would "string" themselves out over a distance as long as a half to three-quarters of a mile. For the most part, all was peaceful until we reached a plateau of dry farm wheat between Jolley's Hill and a watering hole called Last Chance.

New wheat was growing right next to the road without a fence in sight, and the hungry cattle fanned out to graze on both sides of the road. I watched as virtually the whole herd headed for the wheat, except for the two red cows that were walking at the head of the herd. They moved on down the road, ignoring even the tasty grain. To get the herd back on course, dogs followed their masters' signals, some nipping heels, others barking. The loud dogs were usually met with defiance because cows felt their calves were being threatened. Horsemen were riding and yelling. Some had ropes to hit the cattle in order to get them to move, and a few had whips, which popped like rifle shots. Clouds of dust rose, adding to the general discomfort. That we made any progress at all was amazing.

Occasionally a heifer, without a calf, would bolt from the herd and run farther out into those huge fields or into a nearby grove of quaking aspen and sagebrush. While bringing one of these heifers back, I got a view of the entire herd at one time and saw those two red cows still walking down the road, veering neither left nor right.

That evening, after we had put the cattle in a huge corral and were riding home for the night, I asked my father why those two cows were unlike the others. He said that they probably knew where they were going, since they had been to the summer range several times before.

The next day I watched to see what they would do and found they continued the same pattern. They were among the first out of the gate and on the road.

Others followed. When the melee of the first day was repeated, I noticed that the other animals who left the road to eat came back and followed the red cows for a while before going off the trail again. It was then I recognized that the red cows were as responsible for progress as any of us cowboys. They knew the destination and quietly moved toward it. They were not behind the herd barking or at the side of the herd yelling and cracking whips. They just kept walking in front.

In people, this behavior might be called leadership, but actually it is the power of commitment and the effect it has on others. Since then I have noticed that nearly every human organization has its individuals who are tempted from the road, and its attendant barking dogs and horse riders that crack whips. And the most successful organizations will also have those with a vision of the destination, who will continue to live so that those who stray will have a place to return to and move forward again.

When we review our commitments to eternal things, we are granted a spiritual season to see the end, the purpose of our existence. The hope this gives will lighten our burdens and make joyful the passing days. The more we are devoted to righteousness, the more we will be able to know and feel secure in what is yet to come.

Chapter 6

THE
CREATING

There is a story about a prisoner of war in Vietnam who was placed in solitary confinement. Each day for several years, in order to survive, he played a mental game of golf, imagining the course near his home. He would play each hole, stroke by stroke, completing a full eighteen holes. After he was freed and returned home, he was asked to play in a local golf tournament. He was worried that he would play poorly because he had not played an actual game for eight years, but he was surprised when he scored one stroke over par.

Researchers have found that tennis players who watch video replays of their best performances improve more than players who practice without such feedback. Certain instructors in the music department at Brigham Young University require students in beginning classes to read a book titled *The Inner Game of Tennis* by Timothy Galliney. One might question the place of a book about tennis in a music class until it is understood that the author describes how thinking, imagining, and forming an impression of something actually leads to more learning. The music students are asked to forego for a time the rote learning of positions and notes and to play or sing how they imagine the piece of music should sound. The course instructors find that students make more rapid progress if they begin in this way than if they begin with traditional rote methods.

The human mind has a wonderful ability to form impressions. We think about what we find in the world and store it in our brains as images or impressions. To "imagine" is to call up an image, or to form a new one from what is stored in our minds. If we are asked to imagine a tree, for example, we will usually call to mind the kind of tree we have seen most often, or a composite idealized "tree" created by our mind. Once we have formed many internal representations of the outer world, our minds apply what is known to see if the representations match what is outside us. We have, for instance, a profound need to be able to say what we think about something and to have it understood by someone else. Likewise, the goal of artists is to communicate in some "artistic medium" (paint, stone, wood, sounds, words) the internal truths they have derived from their experiences in a way that will connect with and expand the experiences of their "audiences."

While the mind is busy checking its internal impression with the outer world, it often organizes thoughts into unusual combinations. The expression of this mental activity is called creativity. Creative impressions can control our actions, as we saw in the case of the golfer. They can generate better performance than actual physical practice alone. This ability to reorganize abilities by conceptualization has produced great paintings, outstanding scientific discoveries, brilliant musical compositions, beautiful buildings, and prize-winning literature.

Creativity is so highly prized that those who seem especially creative are honored among us. Scientists study the sources of creativity, and people try to generate more of it. Those who have felt it working include race car drivers who call it "riding the flow," which means their minds can anticipate what will soon happen in order to increase their reaction speed. Some painters claim that, while they are painting, a "gnome of the brush" takes over and almost moves their hand to paint while they watch. Athletes tell of playing relaxed so they can "feel" what to do at the right moment.

We have learned that people who are best at it know the same things about being creative. They know it is very personal and follows a style unique for each person. Most insist on excluding others at the time in order to protect their privacy. They are not sure where certain creative thoughts come from. Some appear without much effort, while others come only after several attempts to "get it right." When the impression can be expressed exactly as it was "received," the creative person feels a sense of "rightness" about it. It is so satisfying that most who feel it will rearrange their time in order to increase their participation in it. It is a process many who have known it call divine inspiration.

Most of us think of "creativity" in association with special mental gifts or manual talents. But all of us go through times in life when the desire to create or to generate what is within us and express it outwardly is strong. The time of generation or creativity is a time when we are led into spiritual awareness. Creativity may generally be thought of as inspiration, but only those with a quickened understanding would recognize this time for all that it is. It is a time when our "intelligence," the part of us that has always existed, is revealed from behind the mask of our physical self, and we come to better know who we have been and to form an impression of who we will be. It is a time when we are allowed to know *of* the Father instead of knowing only *about* him. As humans whose ways and thoughts are not like his, we are granted the opportunity to draw nearer to him through our righteous acts of creation. When we experience somewhat what he has experienced, we know of him, for we are, to that extent, like him.

Acts of creation are a routine part of life. People marry and create families. Children are living examples of the need to be creative. We generate the resources to find and beautify homes, plant gardens, or increase our productivity at work. As we grow, many of us fill new leadership positions and enlarge business, civic, and Church programs. When we do all of these, unless our motive is from pure obligation we are responding to the creative urge. We are representing ourselves in the outer world.

Our creations reveal the nature of our own identity. Just as God is known by his creations, so we will be known by ours. Our seasons of creation allow us to discover who we have been and who we will be, thus giving us an eternal view of life.

The Creator's Message

Our creations are representations of our lives as we know ourselves spiritually. It is truly by our works that we are known. If we pay attention to our ideas and subtle impressions when we try to organize or create, we will collect information about our truest spiritual identity. One mother told of listening to some classical music while riding in a car. Her four-year-old daughter began to weep. When her mother asked, "What is the matter, sweetheart?" this child said, "Oh, Mother, it's so beautiful." If women who have given birth are asked to describe that experience, most say they cannot find the right words to fit their feelings. Those who try seldom give voice to the pain (unless it is fresh on their minds). They say instead, "I knew it was the best thing I would ever do," or "I felt as though I had created a marvelous miracle of life."

What do these examples tell us? A young child can respond to beauty and be overcome by it; she might be revealing something about her sensitivity. Mothers create their image in their children. Is there some spiritual longing that is a part of a woman's soul and is revealed at childbirth? I have known women who grieve over miscarriages after only one or two months of pregnancy, as if part of them has been lost. What we are urged to create can tell us about what is innermost. Creators express themselves spiritually through their creations, and those of the same spirit will understand the intent and the message.

An artist-sculptor was selected to prepare some of the statues for the beautiful Relief Society garden in Nauvoo, Illinois. He was a good choice. His sense of beauty had existed and been known by friends since his youth. When he encountered ugly things, especially in human relationships, he was hurt and angry. His spiritual sense seemed to require that all be perfectly at peace. When arguments, discord, or insensitivity were exposed, he often reacted in frustration. The commission to sculpt examples of human relationships was perfect for him. He could place in lasting material a husband and a wife, parents and a child, a teacher and young students, a father and a daughter. Expressions on the statues' faces would, once cast in bronze, remain an expression of love and peace and would affect all who saw them.

He sought models to use and photographed them from many positions. When their natural facial expressions failed to fulfill his idea of the beauty of family love, he could and did rework the clay until expressions were inclined to each other in unmistakable and permanent love. What was within him, perhaps even wholly unknown to him, was finding a representation in his works. His work exhausted him physically, but he was as happy as he had ever been. His soul voice was whispering, and creations of beauty and worth were the result.

When the statues were presented to those who commissioned them, all were delighted. Some were visibly affected as they stood and looked at each in turn. The statues were then shipped to Illinois for placement with some other pieces in the garden. Considerable time was spent planning where the statues would be placed so that the appropriate impression would be made on anyone who visited. A statue of Joseph Smith and his wife Emma was placed first, and others depicting the scenes of love in families were spaced in special ways to convey belonging, solitude, warmth, and peace when families love each other.

The statues had been in place for a few years, and the garden had grown in beauty as the plantings matured, when some graduating LDS seminary students went on a Church history tour across the United States. Most did not know about the garden, nor did they know about the sculptures that had been made by an artist who lived in their home town. Led by adult advisors, the students rode together in buses singing songs popular to Latter-day Saint youth, reading descriptions of what they were going to see, and hearing about the history of each location. This was done so that they might be better prepared as they traveled and visited historical settings of importance to Latter-day Saints.

When they arrived in Nauvoo, it was midafternoon. They went on a tour conducted by the staff of the Visitors Center, and after seeing homes of prominent people from the history of the Church, they were taken to this garden. The students spilled from the bus, and as they walked forward all quieted as if instructed by an unspoken voice. As they walked among the flowers and statues, one after another they began to weep. One, a tall and popular athlete, sat on a bench with his head in his hands, overcome by the spirit of that place.

The artist had delivered his messages even though he had not spoken and was hundreds of miles away. Afterwards, the young people called home to tell their parents of their love and their deep appreciation for spiritual things. If people can understand the artist's message through his creations, it is also possible that all who have made spiritual preparation can, through their creations, express spiritual truth and be understood.

For Us to Understand

We can imagine that our eternal parents want us to "remember" them, to feel after them, and to learn about our premortal time. Our eternal future is affected by that knowledge. We find our parents represented in the organizing of God's creations into planetary systems, in the order of natural law, and in the beauty of the physical world. From these and other creations we can sense the intelligence and the greatness of personality of the creators. These are among the most important things we can ever know. And there is one thing more we can learn, something of great emotional importance. During times of creation in our lives here, we can discover, if we look, in what ways we are significant to our eternal parents.

Children search for parental reassurance of their importance. Spiritually minded people yearn for some interpretation of what special place they occupy in relation to God. Parents have the inherent right and obligation to convey our identity to us, and we are not able to ignore this, whether it is expressed through neglect, abuse, or loving care. Whatever we receive, it will have a lasting impression on us, for we take how they treat us to be an indication of the value we are to them. Some seek answers to prayers in order to discover if God loves them or is aware of them. Some of us sacrifice, and though our gifts are hidden from public view, our secret heart's desire is to discover what the Eternal Father thinks of what we have done. Some seek other means of eliciting a message of approval, such as holding Church positions or rendering service in Church callings. If we are seeking to increase our knowledge of God and hoping to be approved of him, these desires are acceptable. They are all based, however, on the recognition that Father and Mother can, because we are their creation, tell us the place, the purpose, and the significance we have among all their other creations.

By learning of them, we learn of us, and when we deepen our knowledge of us, we deepen our understanding of them. Our season of creation can be, therefore, an exceedingly important spiritual time for us if we choose to see and understand it. When Moses was caught up to a high mountain and talked with God face to face, he discovered that the Eternal Father disclosed himself through his creations. It can be noted that Moses learned his place in relation to God as a result of knowing more of the Father (see Moses 1). These points can be summarized:

God introduces himself:
"Behold, I am . . . God. . . . Endless is my name" (v. 3).

Moses learns about himself:
"And, behold, thou art my son; . . . look, and I will show thee the workmanship of mine hands; but not all, for my works are without end" (v. 4).

"I have a work for thee, Moses, my son; and thou art in the similitude of mine Only Begotten" (v. 6).

Moses is taught about God:
"There is no God beside me, and all things are present with me, for I know them all" (v. 6).

After the vision the glory of God departed from Moses, and he concluded that "man is nothing" (something Moses had never supposed). But God, attempting to have Moses know of his true worth in God's plan, said, "Blessed art thou, Moses, for I, the Almighty, have chosen thee, and thou shalt be made stronger than many waters; for they shall obey thy command as if thou wert God. And lo, I am with thee, even unto the end of thy days." (Moses 1:25–26.)

The prospect of a child's birth is usually a time of excitement. Most use it to learn of the miracle of conception and prenatal development. Mothers feel growth and know physical creation. We dream of the child's gender and what he or she will become. Without our even knowing it, these thoughts are as important to creation as the developing body.

One mother was expecting a child and found the birth pains signaling an immediate delivery. She and her husband rushed to a nearby hospital, and the baby came while the mother was being wheeled down the hall to the delivery room. After parking the car, the father went inside to find his son already born and a little blue. He said quietly to a nurse, "I see he is a little blue." The hovering nurse, in a shrill voice, told him, "Just be calm, just be calm!"

The infant was placed in an isolette to guarantee him enough oxygen. His father, knowing the baby could not visit his mother until morning, stayed by him. During the night, he reached into the plastic arm slots and rested his hands on the baby's legs and back. His time alone with his new son was spent partly looking him over closely to make sure he was perfectly made, and partly dreaming of what this child would be. A nurse wished to know the reasons for the father's close attention. She was told, "He needs to feel that someone is here beside him; he needs to be kept calm." He stayed until early morning, when he knew the baby would soon be placed with his wife to eat, and then he left only after getting the nurse to promise she would caress the baby until feeding time.

What is this child to the father? The father's early experience affected his feelings toward this son, creating protectiveness and care. His experiences with his other children may have created different though equally positive feelings towards them. Later, as this father gives a blessing and a name to his child, he will probably try to put in words what this child means to him. When he teaches his son, watches him grow in school, play in games, and accept the priesthood, the father's feelings will be enlarged, and the exact place this son has in his father's life will be refined. Through ordinations, father's blessings, and countless conversations, this father will tell his son what he means to him, and the son will come to know his place.

Conception and birth are wonderful, but they are only the beginning of the creation of a child. Parents have an opportunity to help create what their children believe about themselves and what they carry into their lives. Whether it is praise or criticism, love or neglect, involved teaching or indifference, parents create a lasting impression for their children.

Some parents I have known set standards that were excessively narrow. One such couple was highly educated, even brilliant. Part of their standard for their children included high academic success. Most of their children were able to meet it, but one of their sons did not possess the intellectual ability to achieve high grades. As a result, he felt inadequate about school. More profound than this, however, he developed a true despair of ever succeeding in life. His failure included low grades plus the shame of inadequacy. His parents placed so much emphasis on academic achievement that all his success in life seemed to depend on obtaining it. When a child is unable to prove himself in a task that parents think to be synonymous with living, he questions the worth of his whole experience.

Attempts by others to point out to him his other talents met with his stony rejection. After realizing their mistake, his parents made efforts to console him. The boy saw this as condescending. He became indifferent to everything except the hurt, the deepest emotion in his life, which was reflected almost constantly in his eyes. He believed his parents did not and could not love him. To him, he was of no worth.

When we discover how susceptible our children are to us, we glimpse something about a parent's creative role. It is this that teaches us what we are to our eternal parents. If we live well, we mortals experience in a measure the life of our eternal parents. In order for us to know them as they are—as loving, caring, and personally acquainted with us—we must treat our own children the same way. By giving our children the hope and security of love and concern, we know spiritually of the hope and security to be gained from parents who love us. This spiritual knowledge comes from our seasons of creation.

Chapter 7

EXCHANGES

_____

His was a story of success. He had been reared all his life as a Latter-day Saint and been faithful in service and belief. His family was bright and beautiful—the good-looking sort that brings admiration. His business was unusually good. He owned a large home, three cars, a boat, a mountain cabin, and other trappings of the affluent. He was well known in his community, having served as chairman of several civic committees.

He was an excellent administrator in his Church calling and was regarded by those closest to him as "one of the great men of the Church." When he spoke, and he was often asked to do so, he motivated and inspired people. One of his favorite themes was that faithfulness leads to prosperity. He looked the living example of this idea. When he said that blessings come from living the gospel, it was easy to see that it was true. In fact, it was said so often and in so many ways that it became the accepted belief. Others in the stake who also prospered added their voices to the idea.

Prosperity was not the central theme of the meetings and programs. It was mentioned just often enough to remind people of its importance. It seemed fitting, even comforting to some, for those who prospered financially to also be prominent. The stake improved under the leadership of these good men, and progress seemed to bring promise of even greater progress.

This apparently ideal situation did not last. In the course of a single year, this man faced serious reverses in his business and had to make sizable adjustments as a result; one of his children had a serious accident leading to permanent disability; another child became involved in a modern sin which was made public and which he found very embarrassing. To all this was added the illness of his wife, who fell prey to the stresses that often accompany misfortune. It did not look as though faithful service brought prosperity. In his speeches he did not say anything more about faith.

Privately, he was angry and felt betrayed. The dreamlike life of yesterday no longer existed. He had been faithful, he thought, truly faithful, and sincere. Why, then, was all this happening to him? There were nights when he would have shed bitter tears had it not been for the tightness in his chest and throat. Despair often prevents its own escape by stopping the release tears would bring. He began to feel embarrassed around the men he met and sensed they noticed his change of financial position. When one had the temerity to ask if help was needed, he politely but proudly refused, claiming that everything was fine.

For a person of religious faith, events like these create confusion not easily cleared. The reasons for our earthly experiences are often unknown to us. From this good and honorable man's experience, his faithfulness had seemed to be the cause for the blessing of prosperity; now it seemed irrelevant. He thought his years of service had earned his blessings. And now, although not willing to admit it to anyone else, he was angry at his religion and his God. Then he was angry at letting himself be duped into believing something which events proved to be untrue.

He was released from his Church calling after honorably completing his time. Unable or unwilling to talk over his situation, he gradually excluded himself from Church activities and in so doing retained his hurt feelings. His mind knew what he should do because he had counseled many others, but his heart would not let him do it. His feelings softened a little, and as the months passed, he had more days that were happy.

He began to read scriptures occasionally, and he was better able to talk with his wife about their situation. While his business had not returned to the successes of former times, it was able to provide an adequate income. The greatest change, however, was taking place deep within his soul. He found that his faith in God was still strong, and he realized that it was his thoughts of the Lord that brought relief from his discouragement. The awakening to this idea was not sudden; it took place in brief moments over many weeks. As his hurt disappeared, his embarrassment for his anger grew, and he sought forgiveness. His prayers became more fervent and his guilt quietly washed away. Peace of mind came, along with more moments when he communed with God and felt whole again. Then he knew that cars, boats, mountain cabins, and prominent positions were not enduring, and all that would endure was his devotion to the Savior and Heavenly Father. Faithfulness, he thought, did bring blessings. It was simply that the nature of the blessings was different from what he had earlier believed.

The events that took his worldly prosperity were forced on him by circumstance. He did not choose and probably never would have chosen this experience. He could have reacted by seeking his former prosperity again. Instead, he concerned himself more about his relationship to God. He found peace that was deeper and richer than anything he had known before. He would never think the same again about what his real blessings were. He exchanged a less than perfect belief for something far more satisfying—the knowledge that God was his friend and loved him. Such knowledge was enduring and made him wiser. The worldly had been traded for the more spiritual. Now he knew that service yielded the satisfaction and calm assurance that God is near and approves.

During the seasons of our exchanges we learn to always reflect on what is true for us. These seasons teach us to rely on that which is lasting, because we find our concept derived from mortality to be insufficient. Even if the seasons of exchange hurt us, we are better for having had the opportunity to discover something better.

The Question

During adolescence, we are so certain of what we think that we commit to decisions and spend the next several years creating a place in the world and building our earthly estate. Then we reach our middle years, a time when many goals have been reached and dreams fulfilled. The pace of life slows. We have less energy. We are wise enough to savor all we can because we know by this time that what seemed to always be available is more fleeting than we thought. The routine we set to achieve our dreams has been practiced for several years both by design and necessity. For some reason, however, our middle years of life allow us to see more clearly that our achievements have come at a price. We gave up some things in order to get what we now possess. The newness of our victories and the pain of our defeats have worn off, and we ask the question, "Is it worth it?"

Some ask themselves this question and find that a small addition like a new experience will fill any emptiness. But the question causes many to soberly review their lives. Some do find a void in their marriages, their life's work, their relationships with children and friends. The resulting lack of satisfaction or balance between what is important and the everyday demands of life leads to the season of exchange when we rearrange time and try to trade what we have been caught in for something we think is better. If we are aware, it is also a spiritual season, a time when we can receive heavenly messages and we can draw closer to what is eternally true.

During this time, perhaps, married people not of the same faith try to accommodate each other. The unbelieving may now wish to be counted among the faithful. Exchanges are made. We seek new employment based on personal fulfillment instead of financial need. Working parents adjust in order to get more time at home. One attorney, for example, announced to his partners that he was going to work 80 percent as much time as he had been and wanted a 20 percent reduction in his income. When asked about the reasons for his decision, he stated he wished to be with his family.

Some career-oriented people have found by this time that work will only produce a limited feeling of fulfillment. What is lacking? Usually they conclude it is the warmth of intimate relationships. They try to invest more in their marriages, perhaps to find the distance of earlier times has forced their partner to create a separate life. For one partner to obtain greater intimacy, both must adjust. Sad to say, marriages often end when one or both cannot adjust. A season of hurt and frustration begins.

The questions we ask ourselves about worth can lead to a revolution in what we believe. Some who are suspicious of people exchange insecurity for trust and find more enjoyment. Some who believed people to be uncaring trade self-pity for assurance. Some who fear public judgment assume leadership and find confidence.

Though our "middle years" are naturally conducive to the process, seasons in which we make exchanges can happen at any time. The spiritual import of these times is usually shown in an exchange of inaccurate beliefs for what is more true and in the improvement of our relationships with others. Truth and increased love are discoveries for those with eyes that see spiritual things during seasons of exchanges.

Exchanging Logic for Inspiration

One of the exchanges people make when they become more spiritually minded is to rely more on the voice of inspiration than solely on the logic of factual knowledge in determining their choices. Missionaries learn quickly that the logical presentation of facts about the Church is not enough to persuade people to alter their beliefs. They find that their investigator must first believe that inspiration is a reliable source of truth before they can become converted to the beliefs of the gospel. It takes great faith to listen to this small inner voice and follow the suggestions. Gaining confidence in it opens the door for more understanding of what God wishes us to know. I was a witness to the way this exchange is made when I had just begun my career as a college teacher.

She was a student in a class I instructed. After class one day she requested an interview to talk about a personal problem. We subsequently became better acquainted and friendly as teacher and student sometimes are. After class one day, she stopped and said, "You are different from my other teachers. How come?" At first I thought she was referring to the way I taught and asked, jokingly, "You don't like the way I teach?" "Oh, that isn't what I meant!" she said. "It's you, something about you."

I told her that if there was something different it was probably because of my religion. Seeing that she was still interested, I asked if she wanted to talk further about it, and we made an appointment. She brought her boyfriend, Tom, who was nice looking and had an assertive and spontaneous personality. We talked about many things, including their plans for marriage following graduation that year. He was a Catholic; she was a Baptist. Neither was very involved in religious activity. She, I was to learn, didn't like some of the beliefs of her church but had strong religious feelings. He knew about his religion but was not religious by belief or by action.

We had several friendly conversations covering many topics, which included our respective religious beliefs. She became more interested; he was quite gracious but obviously less enthusiastic. When our friendship had deepened, I invited them to meet with the missionaries in my home. Both came and participated in all six discussions. Frequently, we felt close as we talked about spiritual things. Not wanting to put pressure on either of them, I made it clear that they would not jeopardize our friendship if they failed to accept my beliefs.

At the conclusion of the last missionary discussion she became involved in a conversation with the missionaries. He leaned to me and said, "Can we still be friends if Carolyn and I do not join your church?" I reassured him that we could but told him, "You should know that you will never be entirely free from the Spirit of the Lord. Once you have heard this message he will follow you throughout your life." "That's okay," he said glibly, and in a short while they left.

We saw each other from time to time and had friendly conversations. The school year ended, though, and we lost contact. She was given a trip to South America as a graduation present and left to visit her friends there. He traveled to Europe to hitchhike around the Continent. The rest of their story is what they told me later.

Her parents were strongly devoted to their religion, and to avoid problems she had chosen not to tell them about her visits with the missionaries. Her father had a violent temper, and she thought it wise not to disturb him. When she arrived in South America, however, she had with her a copy of the Book of Mormon written in Spanish. After settling in, she registered for two classes at a nearby college, which allowed her plenty of free time. On an afternoon walk, she by chance passed the missionary headquarters, and she went in. Coincidentally, she met a missionary who was acquainted with me and they talked briefly. After that she found herself walking many times, each time taking a different route, but somehow always arriving at the same location near the mission home. "I always felt a peaceful feeling," she said, "but I didn't know then why I felt it."

Eventually her life was filled with a round of parties and other social affairs. All was happy and fun. Just before she was to return home in September, a fellow she had dated a few times and obviously liked invited her to go for a ride. She described the episode by saying, "I felt depressed and unhappy as soon as I got into his car, but I went anyway even though I felt I should not." The boy's lack of scruples was shown when he forced her to become sexually involved. Subsequently, feeling dirty and ashamed, she wrote to Tom and ended their engagement without telling him why. She did not want to come home and face him or her parents, so she stayed an extra month.

She did not tell her parents about the unhappy incident, but prepared to work and take some graduate courses at the university. She saw Tom and, despite his protesting, returned her diamond ring, believing that she had "blown everything." Three weeks later the young man she dated in South America phoned her parents saying that he had come to the United States. Carolyn's parents invited him to stay at their home as a gesture of friendship. Unwilling to tell her parents of the ugly episode, she felt forced to go along with their plans.

Meanwhile, Tom had been having some interesting experiences of his own. When he arrived in Europe in June, he did not have much money and began to steal food and clothes wherever he could. He and his friends participated in many things that are part of the licentious elements of society. They covered most of the countries of Europe that summer hitchhiking when they could and stealing enough to get by. Toward the end of the trip he was in Denmark. One night he attended a public lecture about pornography. Tom said, "While I was listening I felt a strong impression that if I did not change my life, Carolyn would not be waiting for me when I returned home." He soon left and arrived home in September, finding Carolyn's letter telling of her desire to break their engagement.

He located his copy of the Book of Mormon and began to read it. One day, looking around his apartment, he noticed the many things he had stolen and resolved to return all of them. It took him several days to complete the task, but he did as he resolved, amazing several store managers. He located a job and then found that his employer was an active Latter-day Saint. He began to attend church, and when Carolyn returned home in October, he told her he was planning to be baptized in November and asked if she would attend church with him. She went with him without her parents' knowledge and said, "I could never pray to find out if the Church was true. I was so afraid of my parents that I read only in the New Testament to learn more about it. But I kept asking the Lord if he would let me know it was not true." She said she noticed a great change in Tom and thought, "Whatever he is doing it must be good." He was baptized as planned and asked her to attend the baptism. She did.

A few nights later, she was assaulted late at night by the young man staying in her parents' home. He left the next day and was never seen again. She was caught now between her feelings of shame and her unwillingness to tell her parents either about the sexual episodes or her interest in the Church. The following Sunday Tom called and asked if she would like to go to choir practice at the LDS Institute near the university. Not feeling wholesome enough to go she declined at first, but later agreed. The choir was rehearsing some parts of Handel's *Messiah* in preparation for a Christmas program. At one point in the rehearsal she noticed a sign in the back on the chapel wall: "Ye shall know the truth, and the truth shall make you free" (John 8:32).

"I am anything but free," she thought, and for the first time she asked the Lord if the gospel was true. "I prayed right in the middle of choir practice, and when I opened my eyes, I wanted to be baptized." Tom told her it was possible. "I went home still afraid to tell my parents," she said. Several days passed, and she was interviewed for baptism, still without telling her parents. The night her baptism was to take place, she finally told them just before Tom was to pick her up. Her older brother met Tom at the door with, "You'll have to go through me to get her." A very angry family argument followed. Her parents finally calmed everyone down, and she left to be baptized.

The next morning her father asked her to leave home. She found an apartment and continued her work. A few months later, she and Tom were married. Since that time they have tried to live their lives according to their spiritual impressions.

He tells of spending so much time in his church calling that he could not follow all the leads given to him as a real estate salesman. He said, "I prayed and told the Lord I couldn't follow all the leads. I was going to place all the cards of prospective clients and select ten. I wanted him to inspire me to pick the most promising." Tom is very successful and believes it is because of inspiration. Carolyn has described inspirational events regarding childbirth and her service in the Church. Both are actively involved and making a good contribution.

In the beginning, neither Tom nor Carolyn had sought inspiration as a source of truth. At first when she received it, she did not obey the impression. Finally, when they did respond to inspiration, they were able to completely change their lives. Their season of exchange brought them truth and love.

Forgiveness

Knowledge of the gospel of Jesus Christ helps us set standards for a righteous life because it gives us an understanding of what we ought to become. The more clearly we understand these standards, the more likely it is that we will live them. To this end, speakers tell us about standards in our meetings. Teachers teach about them in our classes. They are refined and clarified until all are supposed to know them fully.

The standards themselves are, of course, true and helpful guidelines. But because we learn about them by listening, reading, or discussing, they often become more a part of our minds than of our actions. In fact, all humans can *think* of more and better ways to act than they can *live* them. We sometimes focus so much on the destination that we forget we are traveling and the trip is as important as the arrival. This condition creates two false beliefs that govern life for many of us. Some of us are like passengers on a ship bound for a lovely island. During the trip we stay in our rooms looking at maps and dreaming about how wonderful life on the island will be. Our focus on the goal makes us unaware that concerts, lectures, dinners, and other enjoyable things are taking place as part of the trip. Living this way will not only cause us to miss most of what can be enjoyable about life but also it will usually lead us to disappointment when we finally do ''arrive.''

Others of us constantly judge ourselves against the standards of the Church. If we fail to live the standards exactly, then we judge that we are failing. We then feel guilt no matter what we do, because we fail to recognize that the gospel is as much the means by which we can improve as it is the measure by which we evaluate ourselves. The judgments we make often create lasting impressions that are not true. But we will continue to think they are correct unless something happens during the season of exchange that leads to a better truth.

This is seen in the tender story of a lovely woman whose life truly began in her middle years. She was reared in a Latter-day Saint home and was a much-loved child. She was beautiful and petite, with dark curly hair and an olive complexion. Her personality bubbled with a spontaneous sense of humor matched only by an appreciation of the beautiful and fine. She was very popular as a child; everyone in her small town knew her. Attendance at church was a routine part of life. She won awards and took her turn at leadership positions.

There was a boy in her school who was equally attractive and successful. They found each other at age sixteen, too soon for them and soon too intimately. She became pregnant, and her humiliating ordeal began. She undertook the trauma of telling her parents. Marriage followed shortly thereafter. And when the situation became public, her sense of adequacy was severely crippled by the guilt she felt. We do not know if those around her forgave and accepted her. It would not have mattered. Through her anxiety and shame she concluded that a fatal and permanent flaw had been exposed and she would forever be incapable of anything worthwhile.

As she and her husband matured, they had other children and made a successful life for themselves. No one knew of their wrongdoing long ago. No one who knows them would care much even if they did know! It would never have made a difference in anyone's opinion because both are accomplished and loved. But for more than twenty years she was ashamed and felt unworthy and undeserving of any success. She feared social involvement and Church callings. When her children were older she went to college, but she feared failure there.

Her actual record in college was one of accomplishment, but the feelings of inferiority never completely disappeared. Gradually, though, high grades in college and some social successes helped her spirits improve. One day, a prominent teacher of creative writing offered a class at the university. At first, she dismissed the idea of taking the class because, although she loved English, she was afraid she could not write. Her previous successes gave her enough courage, though, and she did enroll. She described the instructor as a master teacher. "He taught me to write," she said, and her voice quavered as the tears began to flow. "I can write," she repeated in a hushed voice. Then, with the resolve of more courage, she said, "I am a person of worth."

For some reason, I suppose, she believed her wrongdoing of long ago must be paid for by self-accusation and the sacrifice of something she wanted to do. Now, because of a master teacher, she had to revise what she had believed about herself. It was a moment of forgiveness when she could at last admit that a single event could no longer prevent her from living what is true about her.

She judged herself at sixteen against a standard that seemed rigidly fixed, and was thereby self-condemned. The standard was not wrong; it was her use of it that was misplaced. She did not understand that, though her act was wrong, she could obtain forgiveness for what she had done. She was traveling on the pathway and was not yet finished. Instead, nothing she did along the way would be good enough because her focus was only on the final destination, not the traveling.

One might wonder about the symbolism of a master teacher and a woman feeling forgiven—a small act of redemption by one who probably did not suspect the full significance of his works. How much greater is the significance of another master teacher who gave his life that we might have a spiritual season to exchange evil for good and find our right path of life again.

When evil is traded for good, we confirm within our souls that an atonement was given us. And through this act of love our forgiveness washes guilt away and makes us once again a person of worth.

Chapter 8

ESTATES

        In the flow of life, seasons
of exchange are often followed by seasons of evaluation and consolidation. We may see the middle life as
a time to view our past objectively, to arrange ourselves to do what is most important. Some use this
season to produce the greatest achievements of a lifetime. Others mellow in order to enjoy what they have
earned. For all, such a season is a time to take stock of
what we have done and what we are doing, and to
start preparing for the next part of life. Some of the
irrelevant and less important details are then elimi-
nated, and greater focus is given to fewer and better
things.

We are less impulsive now and not as likely to get
caught up in things that unbalance our lives. We want
to integrate all parts of life and make the fragments
come together in a way that is comfortable and understandable. Our children may think we are beginning
to speak the philosophical statements of the older, and
hopefully the wiser; but what we are trying to do is
make some sense out of what we see and do, what we
have seen and done.

The same scriptures we have read before have
larger meanings to us now. Words and phrases in our

religious ceremonies stick out in ways that are new. We have climbed to the top of a mountain and are able to see far into the future and back into the past. At the very same moment we look, the young look, and we are aware that we see more than they do. We pause then, trying to fathom the total of the view we see. We contemplate to better grasp the answers, and to our surprise, we feel alone, as if we are the only ones who know.

In some strange way, at the same time that we are integrating our ideas, balancing our time, and using greater wisdom in how we do things, we see ourselves as separate from it all. Sometimes we are frightened and feel the urgent need to seek others and the assurance of their response. Sometimes we catch glimpses that we have been alone in some ways all along and are only now recognizing that we are able to survive and succeed that way. It is the season for the settling of two estates. One estate consists of our wisdom and our possessions. The other is the consolidation and evaluation of who we are and what we have done. Then we turn to face the future as eternity, not just as a few remaining years on earth.

Jesus told of a wealthy farmer whose farms had a yield greater than his barns would hold. His solution was to tear down the old barns and build new, larger ones. After doing this and storing his large harvest, the farmer found he had enough to provide for himself and his family for many years. He said within himself, "Soul, thou hast much goods laid up for many years; take thine ease, eat, drink, and be merry." But God said unto him, "Thou fool, this night thy soul shall be required of thee." Then Jesus said, "So is he that layeth up treasure for himself, and is not rich toward God." (Luke 12:16–21.)

We, too, are in a physical world and have had to acquire physical things. Our estates, large or small, have been created through our sacrifices, risks, and efforts. We have thought often about them, and they are usually a large part of our lives. In our modern day, we are told to plan our estates to prepare for passing our possessions on to the next generation to avoid losing the results of our work. If we think material possessions make up our estate, our legacy will be tied to taxes, legal wills, probate courts, and division of possessions among the heirs. We may have to use our time building bigger barns, spending more time than we want in organizing what we possess.

In contrast, if our estate is made up of the good we have done, our legacy is one of love. This is passed on to our posterity without thought of taxes and courts. In the season of this estate we share many additional caring moments—and we are rich. The gospel of Christ is clear about this point. We are not to value physical things more than we value doing good. When we reach the season of our estates, the truth of this principle vividly stands out. Many who have mistakenly valued their possessions most highly, hope this season is long enough to give them time to catch up on living. Others hope the season is never long enough to express all the love they feel.

The season of life for our estates teaches us the importance of order and organization. Further, these seasons allow us to rid ourselves of the less relevant and to organize what is of greatest worth.

Less Than a Dime, a Nickel, or a Quarter

He was the son of wealthy parents and knew about money. He worked hard himself and, beginning with the opportunities provided by his family background, earned a great deal and was wealthy, too. This was not, however, the central focus of his life. Shortly after his marriage, he learned that he had a disease that could take his life at any time, or could allow him to live indefinitely. It was the sort of thing that flared up occasionally, making everyone think his days were limited, but then would remit. And though he was weakened for a short period, his life continued. Gradually his temperament was affected by all the crises. He was ordinarily a cheerful man, but he became depressed and withdrawn.

For his wife and his children, life with him became unpleasant and strained. His sour moods made for unhappiness. But the greatest cause of his family's sadness came from a false conclusion he reached. None of us knows for sure when we will die, but few would think to prepare loved ones for our death by purposefully remaking ourselves to prevent the development of close feelings. This man, however, decided that distance between him and his family would prevent sorrow at his death. How he created this distance portrays the contrast between love and possessions.

One of his sons explained their family. "Dad," he said, "nickeled and dimed us all the time. If he wanted us to take out the garbage, for instance, he said he would pay us a dime. If he wanted us to get higher grades, he offered to pay us five dollars for each *A* we got. He didn't praise any of us much. He didn't talk much either. None of us were very close to him. We all began to think of how much we could get out of him." The son made his most poignant and revealing statement by concluding, "I didn't feel sad when my father died. I think sons ought to feel something more than loss of money."

While it was too late for this father to love his family, it is not too late for many who enter the season of their estates. There are small kindnesses and gestures of warmth that, like nickels and dimes, add to a great sense of affection. When we look at life with the perspective of this age, we can see that positive time with our families is worth more than any physical possession. It is a more spiritually accurate view than those have who are working to create a temporal estate. We now relish companionship with our children when in earlier days we could absent ourselves from them by working long hours or avoiding them because we were tired of them. Is it because age makes us dependent on them? Or is it that we understand now that families or our closest friends and companions are the basis for our happiness—something wiser people knew all along?

It is as though we are granted a glimpse into a future time and are spiritually urged to settle the estate found in our relatives. We seek to heal old wounds by forgiveness or compassion. One man had disliked a brother for forty years, refusing all the brother's efforts to communicate. He thought this older brother had tormented him so much during their childhood that he wanted nothing to do with him. When a physical examination revealed the possibility of the man's having cancer, one of his first acts was to write to his brother and ask for forgiveness. The stamp cost less than a quarter.

Two other brothers lived close to each other and had a number of painful interchanges during their long lives. They had some harsh feelings following the ending of a business partnership. One, who was brusque in manner, often hurt the sensitivities of the other by what he said. He condemned his younger brother as being an incompetent parent when his child had erred. He criticized his methods at work. However, he later revealed his true character in a humble apology and a request to be forgiven. He settled this estate for less than a dime.

The parents sent their daughter away after she had left their traditional religion. For several years, neither she nor they tried to contact one another. An acquaintance who was on a vacation in the place where the daughter had gone overheard her speaking in a grocery store. After the excitement of the recognition, the daughter asked about her parents. The family friend returned home and told the parents of the chance meeting. Later the parents sought out their child and made amends. Their reconciliation was a joyful way to organize an estate.

Alone

As a young man I often heard and sang the song "No Man Is an Island." Its lyrics extol the ideal of brotherhood, that "no man stands alone; each man's joy is joy to me; each man's grief is my own." It is a wonderful idea that the greatest of all good is accomplished when humankind is bonded together by love and fellowship.

There are some times in life, however, when we are very much alone. I remember the words of a Scoutmaster given on a camping trip. "Moses went on the mountain, alone. Joseph Smith climbed the Hill Cumorah, alone. Jesus suffered in the Garden of Gethsemane, alone. Daniel, the young prophet, stood alone while everyone else bowed to the statue." He was telling us that all of us will find situations that we must face alone, without the comfort or encouragement of another who will perform our tasks for us or make our decisions. We must all, then, prepare to stand alone. We may find it is necessary.

The Scoutmaster did not tell us then that our excitement and growth in life would come from those alone times and that the memories of them would be the most vivid of all our recollections. During the season of our estate, we evaluate our lives by what we have done alone. Other people are around us during these times. It is just that the responsibility falls mostly on us, or the initiative is ours, or we seek or are thrust into leadership. In these conditions, we are alone to do what must be done.

I have read with interest when accomplished people are asked the secrets of their success. I use as examples two successful coaches I admire. I heard LaVell Edwards of BYU say that when he became head coach he knew he would not succeed if he tried to copy someone else. "I knew," he said, "that I had to develop a style of football that I was satisfied with." John Wooden, UCLA basketball coach, said during an interview for television that he seldom talked to his players about another team. "I want our players," he said, "to play our game (his own style) and not worry about what *they* will do." I have wondered if their success resulted from what they were willing to think through and determine alone.

I know a man who has farmed for many years. His farm is beautiful. There are very few weeds on the land. Fences are in fine repair and the soil in excellent preparation. His crops usually have greater yields than do his neighbors'. He is generally regarded as one of the best wheat growers in his area. Over the years, many people have come to ask for his opinion and advice. He is a generous man and gladly shares what he knows. He is a good farmer.

One would think that since he has such a beautiful farm for evidence, everyone would quickly follow his advice. However, some of his advice seems unusual to other farmers, and many are unwilling to try what he suggests. One day a neighbor was about to plant fall wheat. Seeing the good farmer, he said, "Last year I planted the seeds too deep, and much of the grain did not grow. This year I am not planting the seeds as deep." The good farmer scuffed his foot in the soil and found a seed resting in dry dirt. He said, "I try to plant where the moisture is." The man on the tractor did not seem to hear the very advice that would ensure his success. He was concerned about getting his fields planted without making the same mistake he had made the previous year. Now he was about to make another.

After a long, dry summer, many farmers in the area were reluctant to plant until rain had soaked the soil. They waited and waited until late in the planting season. The good farmer was an exception. He planted his grain earlier than usual. Others remarked, "How can he plant when there has been no rain?" He said, "I plant even earlier than usual in the dry years before all the moisture beneath the surface is dried up." The other farmers did not follow his example or his advice. The next year the good farmer had a greater yield of grain than did those who planted late, waiting for the moisture.

The good farmer had developed a method of farming that was his alone. His farm looked as if it was cared for by someone who had taken the effort to think through his methods. What we do on our own for the purest of reasons is the best we will do, even if others do not approve.

Some live following the policies set by other people and do not have as many opportunities to be freely alone. Except for yard care or home decorating, their lives are set in course by the schedules of work, school, and church. Security may be found herein, but some of our growth is limited.

The season of estates, however, usually provides us with the opportunity to do more of what we want. Many look forward to retirement with that in mind thinking they will travel more, rest more, fish more— or simply do nothing. Little do they know that a great adjustment will be required when they are faced with the freedom of time that they alone must fill. Some eventually return to work. Some deteriorate because of the failure to use their time constructively. Others find in this time the exhilaration they hoped would be there. All learn that the freedom of time and the perspective of age present us with what it means to be alone.

When we experience this, we think it to be just another phase we are in. It does not seem that there is anything spiritual about being this old or this alone. In fact, some are terrified by it or resigned to it. It is, however, if we have not found it possible before, the beginning of our own judgment. If we have not had ample opportunity to be alone, we may seek it now as a time to do just what we want. How else will we know about ourselves as mortal beings? Surely not by doing just what is required by others.

I attended a conference at the Spokane World's Fair in July 1974 and listened to President Spencer W. Kimball speak to the presidencies of stakes in the Pacific Northwest. He began his talk by telling us that he had spent several months in prayer and in visiting the temple to learn what he should do during his time as President of the Church. He told that he knew there was something for him to accomplish, and now he was ready to begin. There were many in that room, but I could see no one who was not attentive.

President Kimball went on to tell us that he was to focus on building temples and on missionary work. The work of others has been required, of course, but as the years have passed I have gratefully watched as his statement, ''The day will come when we will see temples dot the land all over the world,'' has begun to be fulfilled. I was a bystander at that meeting and have not been a major part of any of these accomplishments, but if asked I would say he has succeeded at doing what he said was his mission during his tenure of office. He took time to decide what he alone must do. He organized people to do it, and it was done. This work can be used as one way to assess his time spent alone.

Summarizing

Ironically, our evaluation of what we have done as individuals leads us to something different than separateness from others. As if driven by some inner force, the human mind uses the results of our self-appraisal to create summary statements about life. These sound like epitaphs to time. We say them to explain what we have learned about the meaning of life, and we use them to impart this wisdom to others. A young aggressive man would not likely say, "I have learned it is best to worry about what you can do something about and not worry about what you can do nothing about." An older man, after surveying his past, would more likely make such a conclusion.

What is it that seems to be happening when people tell each other of their very different life experiences and find that they have learned the same lessons? People in this stage of life seem fascinated in the telling of their experiences and enjoy finding that another person seems to instinctively confirm what has been said. Are we comparing notes just to see if our own life is strange or understandable? Are we discovering that the mortal experience is one that teaches everyone the same truths? that then, when we reach a certain age, the truth of our individual experience is summarized into a greater or whole understanding by the natural integrative work of our minds?

I remember a story my mother told me about a man born in a far, eastern country. While a youth, his parents taught him that finding the meaning of life was an important thing to accomplish. First, he studied and conversed with great teachers in his own land. Then, having become captivated by his quest, he traveled widely, seeking the philosophers, prophets, and teachers in other lands. Years passed, and he grew old without finding the object of his search. He began his journeying toward home in order to prepare for his death. Arriving by ship, he was heartened to see his homeland. Watching the distance narrow between ship and shore, he realized that he was very happy. Noticing that this feeling was better than any he had experienced in many years, he wondered further at his failure to find the true meaning of life. "Could it be so simple," he thought, "that life is like coming home? that life is whatever I choose to decide it is?" Standing alone at the ship's rail, he came home both to his land of birth and to the knowledge that he himself made up the meaning of life. He could decide for himself what life would mean.

I am confident my mother told this story in an attempt to teach me that joy and happiness came from my own efforts and not from what others supply in terms of wealth, fame, or power. Now though, when I think of this story, I see another moral to it. Not only is our interpretation of life what we choose it to be, but also we are not free to have it otherwise. In his attempt to find the meaning of life, this man ironically made the time of his life into a search for something that was not to be found where he was looking. Until his discovery at the very end, his life was made up of the continued quest without conclusion. In the season of estates, we find that what our own experiences have taught us are, to some degree, also known by everyone else. And what we do not have in common is still revered.

I have wondered if we are to form conclusions so

that we will be able to clearly know what we have learned while here and thus be able to generate the next round of creation. Those who are mortal after us will rely on our experiences, and we will use our understanding to prepare them. This would certainly be true of a God who had mortal experiences and used his understanding to prepare us. Evidence for this exists, I believe, when we summarize life to find its meaning. During the season of estates, we are privileged to summarize what we have learned and still have enough time to enjoy what we know.

Chapter 9

RENEWAL

The school of life does not require that we learn every lesson at a specific time. It does require, however, that we learn all that is necessary for the next life before we enter it. Some people seem to learn faster than others; they go on before the rest of us or live out the years to their fullest. Advanced age tells of the need to catch up on what we have been hesitant about and to review again some of the important experiences of life.

From this vantage point, many who write about ''doing it all over again'' tell us they would take more time to lie on the grass, take their shoes off earlier in the spring, and leave them off longer in the fall. They would take more time to smell flowers and walk among trees. These people's collective message seems to be that, in the midst of taking advantage of each opportunity for growth, we all should enjoy all we can about life.

To those marching in regimental step to the cadence of work and duty, this message seems nice but impractical. Many other messages received from those ahead are likewise disregarded. Then when a new generation arrives at this advanced point in life, they realize that they should have listened more carefully to those who preceded them. They too begin to send messages to the young to prevent them from making the same mistakes, only to find that the sound of the unison steps of the younger generation once again prevent their hearing.

What do the old know about life that the young do not? Is it the clear importance of family, spiritual growth, a certain organization of time, the development of positive character traits? Beyond this, however, advancing age brings life's greatest and most distinct season of renewal. This is a time when we see clearly that life is a *circle of experience*, of bringing ourselves to a fulfillment and returning to life what we have taken; it is the round of eternal life already begun. The end is a beginning. The autumn, rather than signaling the end of summer, is a harbinger of spring. All who know it find courage and hope for what is ahead.

Church members are familiar with the idea that promises made with God and between married people can and should be renewed. When we participate in ceremonies of renewal, however, we often think only of the promise we originally made and how well we are honoring our part. But there is something else that we can think about. When we begin to remember and reflect about something done earlier, we are for the moment turning our hearts back to the experiences that have made us what we are. Remembering these experiences feeds the soul, making it secure and stable in a world of inconsistency and tumult.

Done sincerely and often enough, renewal keeps us faithful as we walk in life's path. Done to inspire our promises, it strengthens our resolve. Done in small ways over many years, it culminates in a spiritual season, and all who do it will know in advance that their existence will not end in death but will always continue. This knowledge that life is a cycle of experience is the harvest in the season of renewal.

The Memories

An older couple came to visit. They wanted to see their child and their grandchildren. The years I have known them have given me many reasons to love and respect them. As I watched them now, I thought that age had only made them finer and more beautiful. He has a natural reserve about him that stimulates respect. His words are carefully measured but have the twinkle of surprise often found in the speech of thoughtful people. He has lived an independent life and been successful. She is exuberant. Her voice is a composition of tones rising and falling with warmth and interest. She has become noticeably smaller as she has grown older, but the expression of her mouth still evidences the gaiety she has known and brought to others. She tells us of their experiences during the winter months in Arizona, the account being interrupted now and then by a small child who dashes by and is stopped for a hug.

As she talks, she repeats the same story as if we have not heard it before. We lovingly listen again, even laughing at the right places. She is not always like this, but more so when she is tired. As dinner is cleared away, our conversation continues. She starts to tell about experiences told twice before, and her husband slightly lifts three fingers off his knee. Noticing, she asks, "Have I told you this before?" We nod to say yes, and then turning to her husband with a bit of exasperation, she asks, "Daddy, why didn't you tell me?" "You weren't watching my fingers," he replied. She laughs, joined by all who have been let in on their secret. We each take a turn telling about our latest activities and then, as usual, the conversation begins to extend back many years to the memories of long ago. Her mind is quick and filled with detail, telling of people and times. She could, if asked, remember a special dress or a special date or something said by a friend long ago.

She was resigned and frustrated a few minutes earlier because she could not remember having just told a story. Now her dark eyes flash and her face lights with the feelings in her memories.

In the short time it took for her to know she could remember something, she has changed. Her age showed when she could not remember. Stimulated by her memories, she is young again, sad again, newly in love again, thrilled with childhood again. As we listen, we feel satisfied to know what her experiences have been. We, of the coming generation, register the facts of her memories because we love her and want to know. But, in the midst of this, she has renewed herself without us giving much notice at all. If she does it regularly, taking it for granted as a natural part of life, then she will know she is eternal. This is the natural function of this final season of renewal. It brings peace, and the uncertainties of the future diminish.

A Personal Honesty

As we grow older, one of the changes that takes place is called *behavioral slowing*. Mental activities slow in differing degrees, depending on our level of activity and involvement. Physical movements slow because of lowered energy levels and the brain's reduced ability to react. Stimulation must be more intense in order to register on our senses, and our senses are less reliable.

When this slowing is excessive, people lose contact with their environment and may suffer emotional disturbance. But, for most, it is a gradual process which we easily grow accustomed to. As a result of it, behavioral scientists believe that one's focus of attention shifts from the external to the internal. Subtle or dramatic behavioral slowing causes us to spend less time thinking about achievements and excitements and more time thinking about the reasons for what we do.

Most of us live with illusions about ourselves, believing something not wholly true. Small or large, illusions are necessary on occasion to protect us against the harshness of self-criticism and the criticism of others. Some of our exaggerated self-concepts are what we would most like to become, and they motivate improvement. When we have time to focus just on ourselves, however, some parts of these illusions are brought into the glare of reality and we see ourselves more honestly. When confronted with a small personal deceit in former years, we might first have attempted to shrug the information away. Then, we may have tried to reduce the discomfort by hiding what we saw in excuses and rationalizations. But now we are less worried about a social image, and our attempts to avoid the truth have less purpose. The facts are allowed to remain, and they puncture us with newfound objectivity. Sometimes we laugh at our foolishness. We hurt at our mistakes. We recognize where immaturity existed within us because maturity did not.

We consider how we have treated people, what we have said, and what we have achieved. There is little left to which we do not give inner scrutiny. The effect of honesty can be substantiated, and it produces emotional states that last long. Discouragement, even depression, is not unusual. Being pleased with ourselves is also possible. These emotions can occupy us for quite a time and may even distract us from seeing that this honesty has a spiritual purpose during the season of renewal.

Those who have faced truth early and often in life will be at greater peace during this time because honesty with themselves has always been more important than an image. But, for those who have lived with some illusion, the honesty of old age is designed to separate us from our excuses and help us live with the exact truth of our lives. This, I suppose, gives contentment to the righteous and a sense of fear to the wicked. Personal honesty is, however, not just a matter of good and bad. It is more a discovery. Prior to mortal birth, spirit beings possessed a personality that had matured and developed. The physical body and the environment of mortal life add a worldly element to this personality. The honesty of advanced age gives us one last opportunity to try to understand what we once were and to live like that here.

I know of a man whose early life was troubled and mostly unhappy. Neglectful and abusive parents had raised him on anger. But in spite of this, the good part of him emerged as he grew, and except for a penchant for sarcasm and cynicism—the effects of his childhood—he was a pleasant person with a reasonably good life. He married, succeeded in his business, and with his wife had several children.

Those close to him suspected that the sarcasm was a mask to cover tender feelings. His wife and children had witnessed poignant moments when his deep feelings surfaced. But he treated these as lapses and quickly covered them by some joke. Recovering, he would resume his facade of granite. His children and wife often yearned for more of his sensitivity and felt they had missed out on the better part of him. As the children grew, married, and left home, their private conversations were sprinkled with ideas about their father's difficulty in sharing himself.

He aged comfortably. He and his wife had a refined and, for the most part, pleasant life. In his
advanced years, he began the practice of having thor-
ough physical examinations twice yearly. Generally
he was in good health, and he kept physically active.
Then, on one of his routine examinations, his physi-
cian spotted something unusual and requested more
tests, which revealed the presence of cancer. So
quickly had it grown that he was given only six
months to live. His first reaction was predictable. He
so resented the unhappy trick his body had played on
him that he made life miserable for everyone.

After he had brooded sullenly about his misfortune
for several days, his wife persuaded him to go to a
seminar about gardening. He decided to go mostly
because gardening had been his hobby for several
years. While there, he heard someone talk about the
way tomatoes can be uprooted to avoid freezing and
hung in a garage or barn, where all the unripened fruit
could be ripened.

For some reason this thought coincided with what
he had been thinking about during the previous days.
He had been uprooted and was not benefitting anyone. Shortly thereafter, he called his married children
together and apologized to them for the way he had
been during their lives and for his actions the previous
month. He wept as he asked for their forgiveness and
told them of his hope that they would be able to share
several happy times before he died.

The next few months were as the family hoped.
Many pleasant gatherings gave everyone a chance to
express the warmth and love that had been absent
through the years. He was living the truth that had
always been within but had been unexpressed. He
and his family knew instinctively that this made him
more like he always should have been. When he died,
there were feelings of sadness but mostly a strong

assurance that their father had performed his mission at last.

The Children

Children and grandchildren are visible assurance that we have extended ourselves beyond our own time. By the time we are old we have seen the power of our parents' traits in us. We are confident that our characteristics have been implanted in our children and see them appear along with familiar family names in our grandchildren. We see that we have imprinted ourselves on others so indelibly as to last forever.

During the season of renewal, we return again and again to our descendants. We hear of their accomplishments, watch their physical growth, and try to assess their spiritual progress. They are the glory of our souls, figuratively and eternally. Our protectiveness and encouragement of them comes about because we see traits and tendencies and can predict what they will do. We try to protect them from the unsavory and encourage them to do well in good things.

We are not unaware of these responses to our children and their children. We talk about those children often because we feel so strongly. It is an easy conclusion to recognize that through this experience we come closer to God, for, as in other ways too, we are like him now as we care for our posterity. No spiritual person will ignore the impressions received about a Heavenly Father during this time. His kindness and his concern for his children are made more manifest because we know of him, feeling as he might feel. We can, as far as we are able, feel his presence across the veil that separates us, and some subtle sense tells us of his love for us.

We are less afraid to meet him then. We have by now carved a body worn and tired, and in our vulnerable moments we wish to be rid of its weight. It is not an unrighteous feeling to wish its removal. It is a spiritual wish to go back from where we came and be renewed. Because of our concern for our children, we know death will be a meeting with this loved Father to whom we feel close. The spirit voice within tells us he is there and he is our friend.

My mother revealed this idea when first learning that the cancerous growth in her body would soon take her life. As we children gathered around her bedside hoping to comfort her, she said, ''I have a friend and He will be with me.'' She had loved her children well, caring for them throughout their lives. When grandchildren came, they were included in her protection and care. She did not forget birthdays. She inquired about each person as she searched for ways to help. She knew of God's love for her because she knew love for her children. She knew of his protective care for her because of her care for others. To her, God was a friend, and she waited peacefully.

The moment of her leaving was similar to the fine moments of her entire life. I had spent the night with her, holding her hand as she fitfully slept while hooked to tubes and an oxygen mask. I sang a favorite song for her, softly, as she stirred and turned. Her fingers on mine were a caress of the love I had felt many times before. As morning came, my father joined us. She clasped his hand and longingly looked into his face. A hushed sound came from her lips and she left. We think, to meet her Friend. She renewed herself by returning to the one who sent her.

Chapter 10

THE
LAST
SEASON

"I am going to die," she stated matter-of-factly. Having learned from other experiences that someone with a terminal illness does not always benefit from sympathy, I replied quietly, "So?" Her eyes danced a bit, and a smile flickered at the corners of her mouth. "Dying is very serious," she said in the way one would ask the time of day. Not knowing what else to say, I blurted, "How one lives seems to be more important." To my surprise, she smiled and said, "That's why I am here. Knowing that I am going to die is on my mind, but there are many things about living that I do not do well and are not as I would like them. I want to have things just right before I go." Through her I learned that dying is a spiritual season with lessons to be learned. It is a welcome back into the existence which is more real than life here.

She was slight of build with dark hair and eyes; she was given to a quick smile, and the corners of her eyes had humor etched in them. I was to learn that she could think deeply about complex subjects, quickly form conclusions, and raise questions that were difficult to answer. Her voice was soft, and never in our acquaintance was it filled with anger. The most she ever showed was frustration or impatience. Her name was Lynne Mathews. She was married, and the mother of seven children.

After she left that first time, I thought that more people ought to think about dying. Maybe it would help us to think about how we are living. I drove home that evening with renewed appreciation for the idea that those who know they are soon to die understand more clearly the difference between what is important and what is insignificant.

People who know in advance that they are going to die are faced with a concentrated version of what all mortals face. Their foreknowledge, however, forces them to think about death in ways that others do not. From them, we can see that facing death is a season of particular spiritual abundance. Dying is more than the termination of mortal life as we know it. It is a beginning of some other existence.

While Lynne's disease made its relentless progress from one stage to another, we had a series of long discussions exploring the meaning of things, adjustments that could be made, and the nature of the existence after mortal life. Sometimes she would just show up and ask, "Could I talk to you for a few minutes?" This meant she had thought of something and wished to share it, or she wished to ask me a question. She was always welcome.

I wondered if she would one day dissolve into a pool of tears, complain of the pain, or criticize the discomfort of a medical treatment that was not helping much. She never did any of these. The only tears she shed were because of truth discovered or expressed love for her husband and children and gratitude for the wonder and beauty of just being alive. Her only complaints were about her inability to make herself do all that she wanted to do. And instead of criticizing her doctors, she learned to appreciate their limitations, concluding that when all else was said and done, rather than be hospitalized she would prefer to face her future by herself and with the people she loved. She would find that facing her future was endurable if she had the companionship of others.

What Dying Teaches About the Meaning of Life

Looking back, I should have known that any discussion about death would inevitably lead to a discussion about the meaning of life. But, being new to the task of helping someone prepare to die, I did not know what to expect. When Lynne began to ask what life is, it seemed such a broad area that I did not, at first, know how to approach answering it. I hoped, in fact, that she would forget about it so I wouldn't seem unprepared. But she persisted in her questions, and I felt increasingly obligated to come up with something that might be useful to her.

One day while thinking about her, I recalled an incident recorded in the Book of Mormon. It led to something I eventually discussed with Lynne. The event, familiar to most Latter-day Saints, was the brother of Jared's witnessing the spirit body of Christ, and being astounded by that revelation. After learning the truth about the identity of Jehovah, he was almost immediately shown a vision of the history and future of this world and then told to seal up the record. I wondered, "Why, after learning about Jehovah, was this man shown this particular vision?" I thought of other similar situations, when Moses and Abraham, for example, were taught about God's numerous and heavenly creations. I concluded that knowledge of God is necessarily followed by increased knowledge about oneself, and the Lord's method of teaching is to show how a person fits into the total scope of life on earth. If this conclusion is true, then mortal life is designed to help us discover the true nature of our own souls.

Armed with what I thought would be a good answer to her questions about the meaning of life for Latter-day Saints, I felt ready to talk at our next visit. After telling her of my conclusions, I was surprised when she did not seem satisfied and continued to ask what mortal life was. She seemed to be asking not only what mortal life is but also how she could best use it. Because she was dying, she knew that her time in mortality was limited. It made a lot of sense, therefore, that she was worried about how she was using her time. At least in the season of dying, one clearly evaluates every minute. "How do you decide what is right?" she asked. The look on her face asked for more than the traditional answer of study, prayer, and thought. She was asking about everyday styles of parenthood, ways of treating people, or ways of spending free time—all the areas of life that we seem to fall into and develop habits for.

Although I had not ever given much thought to the matter, I could very clearly see that the time of mortality makes doing what is right as often as possible a logical necessity. It was not simply a matter of religious values learned from Church and parents. If there is a specific amount of time allotted to us, then we should want to know how to use it best. To do "right" is to fill time usefully. The term *useful* only makes sense if there is a purpose to our existence, a place we are working to find. "Right" is what "usefully" prepares us for that place; "wrong" is what does not. Lynne wanted to know how she could know what was right in all areas of her life.

The nature of life, I pointed out, was such that while there are some things we all must do in an exact way (like baptism, for example), there are numerous other things not prescribed for us. All of these are curious in one respect. They have both good and bad properties. For example, a woman who thinks that a very clean and orderly house is the "right" thing to have, may in the cleaning effort limit the time she has with her children. Or one who tries to learn many things may miss the depth and extent of achievement she would experience if she were to focus on only one or two areas. This paradoxical characteristic of mortality is the foundation of freedom. So it is not that any of these things are exactly "right" or "wrong." The right thing for us to do is to recognize our inherent responsibility to make a *choice*. How clean a woman keeps her home is not as important as whether she responsibly chooses between alternatives, knowing that some desirable and some less desirable things will result. She must, as must all, realize the consequences of the choices she has made.

"I think I understand what you're saying," Lynne responded, "but how do I know if the way I choose to run my house is right for me?" "Well," I answered, "if you have actually decided to make a deliberate choice about what is 'right' for you to do, then it is important to try to choose the alternative that will yield the greatest rewards to you. You must try to determine whether you have responsibly decided for yourself or whether you have coasted along on the traditions of your mother, other people, or your own habits."

She acknowledged that many things she did were not the result of thoughtfully making her own decisions. "Then," I pointed out, "you are not doing the 'right' thing. You are merely coasting instead of thinking it through and responsibly deciding what is best for you."

"But there must be a way to know what is right,"

she insisted. I proposed to her that since the scriptures clearly indicate a premortal life for us prior to coming here, it was likely that we knew those premortal laws before we were born. Once mortal, however, we became susceptible to tension, temptation, anger, and other conditions that might hinder us from abiding eternal laws. The gospel is the only set of laws that allows us to live successfully in a mortal world and still prepares us for what is to come. For example, the Savior taught us to live in obedience so that we may be partakers of peace, love, his rest, and the stillness of soul that true knowledge of him requires. People who do not follow his laws will not live in peace.

Having made that point, I suggested to her that the purpose of mortal life was to live so that we could practice or rehearse the laws governing the eternal world. "What is the profit," I asked, "if a woman has a clean home, and at the same time fills her family and herself with the tension and frustration of mortality? That seems contrary to the laws governing the world of spirits or exalted persons." I asked her this question because she had pointed out that she put too much pressure on her children to keep things clean and organized.

"If I were living 'right,' " she replied to my question, "then I would live here so that whatever I did would not prevent me from feeling peaceful and calm. If people who live in a postmortal life live with love and peace, then I must practice feeling those feelings here so I will not find them foreign to me and be uncomfortable there." This is how she decided what was "right" for her to do.

Body and Spirit

I have come to know the importance of true principles that are steadfast and firm across the span of this life, extending into worlds and existences we have yet to know. I am certain that these places and times exist, that this life has a purpose and preparation. And further, the requirement to know that what we do here can determine what we are to become there presses upon my mind with a confirming assurance. I occasionally have small doubts that these things are true. But most often, I believe I need to make choices about how this life will influence me in order to live so that I can prepare to die as well as my friend prepared.

In Lynne's case she had to hurry. Her time was limited, and she wanted to get as much of her life in order as she possibly could. Once she came to this realization, she examined her life as a wife, mother, homemaker, neighbor, church worker, and friend to ensure she had made her own decisions about them.

The more decisions she made, the less she depended on me for answers. She gradually changed her orientation and just informed me of what she was doing. She also began to inform the Lord, explaining to him what she was going to do and why. She did not wait to be told; she became "anxiously engaged" in doing her good because, I think, she understood that it was the act of choosing and doing what was "right" for her, and having it confirmed by the Lord, that would help her be a valiant daughter of God.

Though her body was gradually weakening, it would have been apparent to anyone that her spirit was gaining strength. She seemed, except when physically limited, to be more committed to getting important things done. She looked as though she were actually more definite and energetic. I felt I was an observer of the way a person overcomes the influence of mortal flesh. She, or at least the everlasting part of her, was not dying. That part was growing. As a result, it seemed clear to me that a time would shortly come when she should, and would, want to discard her body because it was restraining her—a burden, a physical hindrance to the progress of her spirit.

Interestingly, she seemed unaware of it all and did not notice it until just before her death. But I could see it, and I was awed by it; so clearly was it portrayed that I truly felt I was witnessing an event that would ordinarily take place over a long period of time, but was now collapsed into a microcosm made vivid by its rapidity. Every day she was more advanced spiritually than the day before.

I had read accounts and known of some people who demonstrated remarkable spiritual presence. But nothing I had ever read was as invigorating as what I was observing here. I began to look forward to seeing her just so that I could participate in watching some-one's spirit clearly emerge as the champion in the age-old contest between spirit and flesh. Mortal life became for her a time of exacting every good memory, seeking every good feeling, seeing what was beauti-ful, and sharing love with loved ones. All focus on the body was gradually left behind.

Faith and Hope

Lynne's life had become a process of experiment-ing with and exploring the familiar. Feeling somewhat removed from the normal pace of life because of her illness, she began to notice and think about things so common as to ordinarily warrant little attention. She talked about mundane things such as taking a child to music lessons and waiting for her. We reviewed the importance of having a clean house, as opposed to one that was not so neat and tidy. She told of times when she had nagged her husband about the weeds that needed to be pulled. She talked of conversations with a school principal about the best situation for her youngest son. She explored some elements of her marriage, and occasionally brought her husband to our discussions, inviting his participation. She wondered about her competence as a mother, and reflected about a statement or a mannerism, wishing to know whether a certain disciplinary technique was more effective than another. She renewed her memories of each small part of life.

Gradually, too she began to see her death as part of these experiences. Dying, as it turns out, is one of life's events. As Latter-day Saints believe, its purpose is to alter the form of our identity in order for us to end one period of our progression and begin another. Death has a purpose, and we can face it, even when it appears to be "untimely." Death will be a part of everyone's life.

Lynne liked this idea. Her dying had seemed forbidding because we knew little about it, but both of us knew of stories of people who had had a near-death experience and reported that it was not a bad thing. Perhaps, then, I proposed, death can be something we can eventually look forward to. After I said this, or something like it, she looked me squarely in the eyes. I felt that I had slipped into some sort of trap and was waiting for the clanging of the door to seal me in. But she sighed and was silent. I thought she must be thinking: *What do you know? You are not facing death.* In order to escape the trapped feeling, I suggested that she was fortunate because she had time and could do it "right." She laughed, releasing the tension. "You have the knowledge of impending death," I told her. "You can use your freedom and the Lord's inspiration to determine what purpose it will serve. You can think about how you would like to have lived the next year, and then do it now. Make your dying accomplish a useful purpose for you.'' It would take a commitment based on her faith.

I have thought since then that this idea was the most important one we discussed. How truly remarkable that we, with the Lord's help, can choose what purpose some event will have for us. I thought it a bit strange at first, but some examination of it has made it more exciting. We can have faith that even though we may not be able to choose all that happens to us, through knowledge of the gospel we can work to determine the purpose of an event and use it for our benefit. We don't have to worry about the cause of or reason for something we find hard to understand.

I believe this is when the Lord is truly involved with us. His spirit seems to echo the whisper, ''Go on. Keep going. You'll find the way.'' By squarely facing the future and moving toward something we hope for, we can make life's events full and satisfying. With this thought, I began to recognize for the first time in my life why hope and faith are necessary if we want to progress and become exalted. These spiritual attributes are found in all our acts of creation. It surprised me to see how significant and real these intangible substances were for Lynne Mathews. Because she had hope, she could use knowledge of her impending death purposefully and usefully to create good up to the very moment she died.

From this point on, she began what came to be a deep reexamination of her marriage; she wanted to make sure that she and her husband were doing everything that would bring them an eternal life together. The amount of love they shared, her husband's style of leadership, their parenting skills, her ability to understand and be sensitive to him—these were things she brought up in our discussions. She talked about her children and asked about ways she could make her relationship with each of them as happy and as lasting as possible.

She exchanged her attention on the mundane of this world for a focus only on that which would be everlasting, intangible things such as love and faith. She examined her actions as mother, wife, and friend to see if she was doing them "right." Now she talked about the emotional or spiritual aspects of them, rather than the physical.

Going Home

I can now see the connection between the attention she gave to intangible or spiritual things and what was to come. Her physical body was dying, but she knew her spirit was going on. It seemed to me that without conscious thought on her part, her spirit was becoming ready for what she could encounter at death. Her request to discuss this topic was not motivated by a fear that some people have at death, trying to discover God in order to avoid punishment for their sins. Her reason now was similar to that of someone going into a far country and wanting to know about the people who live there. Because the question seemed so natural for her, without her awareness of anything unusual, I was struck by its significance.

Usually, as we talked, it was my custom to use examples from other people's experiences in order to help clarify a point we were discussing. I found, however, that using experiences of others now did not satisfy her. One day as we talked, I used a scriptural reference as an illustration. Her face relaxed. She reflected thoughtfully. It would have been apparent to any observer that I had found the language in which she wished to learn as she tried to understand what would happen shortly to her. Not only did she wish to know about her relationship with God but also her spirit seemed to request that we use a means of communication that was more comfortable and useful than earthly language. The scriptures conveyed something that my logic and examples did not. In the pauses that are part of any conversation, I could thereafter see her soul grasp an idea or a meaning that could not be spoken just as tangibly as if my eyes had seen a tree, car, or house.

From that time on, we talked using two levels of communication. One level included the words and sentences that are part of the reasoning common to our language. The other level was something sensed without words. The image, impulse, or impression of something we were discussing was richer and more complete than separate words were able to convey. I remembered Nephi's comment that he could not write or speak about what he had experienced. I believe that I knew somewhat of his feelings. When Lynne and I understood each other and understood the truth, we both knew it simultaneously.

This form of communication between us continued until she was unable to come for her visits. After several weeks had passed without my seeing her, I received a telephone call from her. She told of having been in a deep coma that ended at exactly the same moment her family and ward ended a fast in her behalf. She said, "I don't know where I've been, but it is a lot better and more refined than this place. I am anxious to go." She then asked if she could come and visit. I assured her of my desire to see her, so her daughter brought her. Her body was obviously at the end of its usefulness. Her face was ashen gray. She was thin and weak, but deep within her eyes there was a "knowing" or confidence I will never forget. Her visit was brief. She asked if I would speak at her funeral. I agreed, and asked only if she would be present. "I'll try," she smiled.

I never saw her alive again. Two or three weeks later her husband, Jim, telephoned me to tell of her death. One morning, he said, she had called for him, and she left this life while lying quietly in his arms.

She had prepared a lovely funeral. Relief Society sisters provided the opening music; her neighbor Jeffery Holland and I spoke. All seven of her children sang the beautiful song by Phyllis Luch and Jeanne B. Lawler:

> I often go walking in meadows of clover,
>   and I gather armfuls of blossoms of blue.
> I gather the blossoms the whole meadow over,
>   dear Mother, all flowers remind me of you.
>
> Oh, Mother, I give you my love with each flower
>   to give forth sweet fragrance a whole lifetime through
> For if I love blossoms and meadows and walking,
>   I learn how to love them, dear Mother, from you.
>
> *(Sing with Me, D-15.)*

Lastly, her husband spoke, giving a loving description of how he and his wife had met. The many who were in the chapel were filled with love. I believe she was nearby. She had finished her last season with grace, faith, and dignity, and in doing so had taught many how to do it "right." I will always love and respect her.

From all I have seen, and my understanding of it was confirmed and expanded in my association with Lynne Mathews, I have come to believe that the capacity to understand spiritual things is built into us from the beginning of our lives; and our spirits knew and followed truth before birth. Unless our manner of living is dark and spiritually indifferent, a set of impulses will naturally occur during our lives to help us recognize eternal truth. Those who so live as to give place to these seasons of the spirit, will add to their knowledge of truth and to their ability to govern themselves according to it, until they can forever be where God is, because they are like him, having been nourished by an inner spiritual sense.